COLORADO PLACE NAMES

Communities/Counties/Peaks/Passes

WITH HISTORICAL LORE AND FACTS
plus
A PRONUNCIATION GUIDE

by Geo. R. Eichler

Foreword by
W. E. Marshall
State Historical Society of Colorado

JOHNSON PUBLISHING COMPANY
Boulder, Colorado

Library of Congress Catalog Card Number 77-089726
ISBN: 0-933472-26-9

Excerpt from the poem *Report of My Strange Encounter With Lily Bull-Domingo* by Thomas Hornsby Ferril, copyright 1966, used by permission and courtesy of the author.

Excerpt from the song *C-Oh! Hello! Hooray! D-Oh!*, words and music by Roscoe K. Stockton, copyright 1926, used by permission and courtesy of Paul and Oakley Stockton.

All photographs are of Colorado scenes, courtesy of the State of Colorado Advertising and Publicity Department. Cover: Long-abandoned mine structure at Governor Basin with Mt. Potosi (13,790 ft.) in background, near Ouray.

JOHNSON PUBLISHING COMPANY
1880 South 57th Court
Boulder, Colorado 80301

CONTENTS

Dedicated to
The Memory of My Mother and Dad,
Katherine and Gustave R. Eichler,
who went westering from Brooklyn—not trail-blazing pioneers but neither Johnny-come-latelies—when Colorado, the state, was little more than a quarter-century old; to proudly settle and add their names (and later mine), to the rolls of a magnetic and colorful land.

FOREWORD

Most of us delight in travel and part of the fun is learning about what we see, or telling others what we know. Historic and patriotic organizations erect markers about what was; chambers of commerce tout local wonders, entrepreneurs entice with billboards of opportunities that lay ahead, visitor centers dispense leaflets portraying multiple choices on how to spend our time and money, maps are valued for the diversity and accuracy of the information they contain, and for the really thorough, there are the State guides prepared during the depression by teams of writers and historians.

What we call our towns and counties, our mountain peaks and our passes, is fascinating, and now we have *Colorado Place Names* to enrich many an otherwise weary mile.

The names across Colorado stimulate the imagination, recalling the Native Americans who lived with the land, Arapahoe, Ouray, Saguache; reminding of French trappers whose solitary wanderings left a mark, Poudre Park, Platteville, Dumont; echoing Spanish explorers and settlers, Sangre de Cristo, Trinidad, Las Animas; honoring heroes, Kit Carson, Custer, Moffat; revealing the pioneer sense of humor, Punkin Center, Mosca, Paradox; heralding the part the Army played in settlement, Fort Garland and the other "Fort" towns; romanticizing the west, Wild Horse, Rifle, Wagon Wheel Gap; revealing the homesick, Ohio, Texas Creek, Akron; commemorating our mining history, Bedrock, Coaldale, Silverton, and a silver capitol called Leadville; celebrating the hopeful, Prospect Valley, Fairplay, Climax; and, scattered everywhere, the descriptive, Saw Pit, Castle Rock, and Stonewall.

Our places were named stolidly and romantically, with hope and despair, and George Eichler has organized most of our place names into one handy package for a trip through Colorado, by car, or by imagination, without leaving home.

W. E. Marshall
Executive Director
State Historical Society of Colorado

A Note About Pronunciations

Colorado has a "melting pot" mix of name originations. There are names by and for: Indians, Spanish explorers, Spanish-American settlers, English, French, and American trappers, miners, settlers, railroaders, etc.

Because of the many possibilities, a phonetic pronunciation guide is given for many of the communities, counties, peaks, and passes. These are shown immediately following a place name, within brackets, and in italics.

Much depends, however, who is doing the pronouncing. In a given community the Spanish-Americans or "old timers" may say the name with a Spanish pronunciation, while others may employ a "modern" version.

Often the accepted pronunciations result in a mixture. Rio Grande, for example, is usually spoken as "Ree' oh-Grand'," (River Grand). The pure pronunciation is "Ree' oh-Grand'-aye." (When speaking of the stream, Rio Grande, avoid redundancy: don't say Rio Grande River.)

An effort has been made to reflect, in the phonetic listings, the generally accepted local usage. However, despite searching out authoritative assistance (including Floyd Baskette's most helpful guide), some towns' pronunciations still have no concensus.

Incidentally, Colorado is always spoken as "Kahl-uh-rad'-oh." Inhabitants of the state are Coloradans (Kahl-uh-rahd'-uns): Drop the final "o" and add an "a" and "n."

INTRODUCTION

C-Oh! Hello! Hooray! D-Oh!
I'm a mile high feelin' fine!
'Cause I just got back
To my mile high shack,
In this healthy, wealthy,
Wonderful state o' mine!
As I Stop! Look! Listen!
Not a hill top's missin',
And the sun just loves to shine!
It's C-O! L-O! Hip-Hip-Hip R-A-D-O!
Tell the world I'm feelin' fine!

from: "C-Oh! Hello! Hooray! D-Oh!"
by Roscoe K. Stockton.

The songwriter parenthetically termed his lilting tune "the mile-high *spell* of Colorado." It sums up the feelings most natives—and probably most of the new-permanents—have for the colorful state.

As one of the United States, Colorado was number 38, being given statehood on August 1, 1876; the only state to be admitted just one hundred years after the Union was established. Now it has observed its own centennial and the nation its bi-centennial birthday.

As this is a book of place names concerning Colorado, the state's name probably should be discussed first.

The name—for the Colorado River—is one of the oldest in the country, dating back to 1604. Spanish explorer Don Juan de Onate used it for the river, as its waters ran nearly red—which is the literal translation of the word: Colorado: Color red.

The rugged country that is now Colorado, the state, had not then been completely explored along the upper reaches of the Colorado River. The Territory of Colorado (1861) took its name from the stream.

Later it was determined that the original Colorado River did not flow within the state's boundaries. It took a long time for a solution. This came by changing the name of the Grand River, eastern branch of the Colorado, from Grand to Colorado. The change became official in 1921, making the Colorado River the same name from its headwaters near Lulu Pass, above Grand (not Colorado) Lake.

About the state itself: Centennial State, Colorful State, Columbine State, Mile High State—all are quick but insufficient descriptions. (And Denver advertising agency Broyles,Allebaugh & Davis posted billboards in the 1960's with the suggestion: Smile . . . You live in Colorado.)

Irene Pettit McKeehan, writing about "Colorado in Literature" in, *Colorado: Short Studies of Its Past and Present,* published by the University of Colorado in 1927, cites a description of Colorado as one of the best she had ever read.

The quotation is from Hamlin Garland's *The Forester's Daughter*, published in 1914:

"There are two Colorados within the boundaries of the state of that name, distinct, almost irreconcilable. One is a plain (smooth, dry, monotonous), gently declining to the east, a land of sage-brush, wheat-fields, and alfalfa meadows—a rather commonplace region now, given over to humdrum folk intent on digging a living from the soil; but the other is an army of peaks, a region of storms, a spread of dark and tangled forests. In the one, shallow rivers trickle on their sandy way to the Gulf of Mexico; from the other, the waters rush, uniting to make the mighty stream whose silt-laden floods are slowly filling in the Gulf of California.

"If you stand on one of the great naked crests which form the dividing wall, the rampart of the plains, you can see the Colorado of tradition to the west, still rolling in wave after wave of saw-tooth edge. The landscape seems to contain nothing but rocks and towering crags, a treasure house for those who mine. But this is illusive. Between those purple heights charming valleys wind and meadows lie in which rich grasses grow and cattle feed."

Other than quarreling with the words "humdrum folk" the precis is a good one. Substitute "adventuresome" for humdrum—because surely it's all that—and it's excellent.

So much for the state itself. About the communities, counties, peaks, and passes, these names—and their origins—are commented upon in the separate sections to follow.

Shakespeare said it (in Romeo and Juliet): "What's in a name? That which we call a rose / By any other name would smell as sweet."

Everything seems to have a name, animate and inanimate. So it's interesting that with everything so designated, there still is a fascination about names and their origins. True, particularly of given and surnames, and the communities in which we live.

In *American Place Names*, George R. Stewart—also author of the classic *Names on the Land*—points out there are an estimated 3,500,000 named places in the United States, plus another million names recorded but no longer in use.

By simple division this means about 70,000 names per state; undoubtedly high for the less heavily populated states such as Colorado. Still, one federal agency is gradually putting together a gazetteer for Colorado which will have an estimated 40,000 names—including natural features. (The compilation is years away from completion.)

This book of *Colorado Place Names*, then, is really a small fraction of all the Centennial State's toponyms. However, it does cover all the names of communities, cities, towns, settlements, junctions, etc. shown on the official Colorado Highway Map—some 600 separate listings—published by the Colorado Department of Highways. The word "official" is stressed because all named settlements and junctions do not appear on all maps (including the official state map). A few names not showing on the official map have, however, been included in the roster.

In other sections of the book are the origins of the names of Colorado's counties, the 14,000 ft. peaks, and the major highway passes. The peaks and passes are indexed on the official map, the counties are shown on the map itself.

Using the index on the official map, each named location can easily be found using map's quadrants. Obviously, the book's use does not require using a map in conjunction. However, particularly for travelers who are using the map, this book will make a trip more enlightening and (hopefully) more rewarding.

A note of caution for travelers. The word "communities" is used broadly. A small number of named places are no more than road junctions; some have, in the past been settlements—others have not. And a few are now so-called ghost towns (in name only). This is only to suggest that a traveler should not depend on this book (or the state map) alone for locating possible shelter, food, or fuel.

Listed with the communities are other interesting facts, including, in many instances, populations. According to the notes of the 1970 U.S. Census of Population, the census included all incorporated and unincorporated places of 1,000 or more. Those of lesser population were listed by county subdivisions. In other words, some communities plus other areas might be totalled, population-wise, together.

Unless separate population figures were shown for each community name, none is given in this book, although most settlements do have some population.

G.R.E.

COLORADO'S COMMUNITIES

Looks like we got us a town, boys,
So what'll we name this place?
Let's get our burgh on to the map
And put 'er right into the race.

Could be our town will grow to a city—
Should that be part of the name?
Let's get a name for our town, boys.
Let's get 'er into the game.

from: "The New Town."

The fascination and curiosity about place names is widespread. It's odds-on that even before these words are read the reader has skimmed the pages to discover the origin of a particular name or two that he's wondered about. Great.

What started out as a seemingly simple project turned out (as most projects do) to be somewhat complicated and complex. And though every name indexed on the official Colorado Highway Map has its origin cataloged here, some are of obscure definition.

In January, 1940, *The Colorado Magazine*, published by the State Historical Society of Colorado, began printing a series of the state's place names. These lists, which included no longer existing towns, were prepared by the Colorado Writers' project of the Works Project Administration. The WPA was a federally-funded program to help stimulate the economy (and make jobs) in the years following the 1930's depression.

A majority of the name origins were taken from this little-known but valuable source. Others were researched in the Colorado Historical Society's Library, the Denver Public Library's Western History Department, countless books, newspapers, and personal correspondence with out-state libraries, historical organizations, and cooperative, helpful individuals.

Few name origins have been officially recorded, and those which have been are mostly for communities which have become incorporated entities. The origins recorded by the WPA writers were based on personal recollections of early settlers or residents and/or their descendents, from correspondence with local officials (frequently postmasters), and incomplete records and notes.

Beginning—or the end—of an early mountain mining town.

Therefore, many origins given here are open to question; often two or more versions exist. This uncertainty applies, as well, to some of the 150-200 origins this compiler obtained from various sources.

In order to make the end results as useful as possible to as many users as possible, the year of each community's founding or establishment has been included. Where incorporation exists, this is shown, plus official 1970 U.S. Census Population, a bit of local history, and in some cases, a phonetic guide to pronunciation.

Usually, where an incorporation occurred, the year of the town's founding was among the data. Most of these dates (years) came from the useful—but no longer published—*Year Book of the State of Colorado.* The same source supplied many of the founding dates for communities not incorporated.

But whatever the source, the year of a settlement's establishment often is unanswered completely—and all are subject to different criteria (apparently) by the founders. Some towns date from the first settler's homestead around whose farm or ranch a community eventually sprouted. Others date from the filing of a formal town plat. The establishment of a post office frequently was the signal for a "formal" settlement, and so on.

For all the communities listed herein, the year of founding follows an accepted source in most instances. When an exact date could not be determined, then what appears to be the founding year is followed by a question mark. With some only an approximation could be reckoned and the date given is used with "circa." In a small number of listings the date of the first post office has been given in lieu of other firm facts. The latter is shown as P.O.E.

Colorado's geographical location has been a factor in the wide variety of name sources. In the southern part of the state many of the names were given by the Spanish or their Mexican descendants. Indian names—from a number of tribes—are found in all parts of the state. The coming of the railroads brought many names—for men (and sometimes women) in some way associated with the iron horse—and not a few names are linked to the promoters of land and towns adjacent to the railroad tracks.

Explorers, scouts, Army personnel as well as pioneering settlers all are among those whose names dot the state's towns.

Some of the different or unusual toponyms include a town named for a little girl (Farisita), for a blacksmith (Weston), for a popular song of the times (Red Wing), for a mountain bird—the jay (Camp Bird), a prehistoric reptile (Dinosaur), for rock hounds (Gem Village), a comic strip (Toonerville), a flour mill (Molina), and a brand of flour (Marvel), a vegetable (Punkin Center), and an insect (Yellow Jacket), just to call attention to a few.

Key: Community, County, Established, Incorporated, 1970 Population. P.O.E. signifies Post Office Established; C indicates circa. Phonetic pronunciation is shown in italics, in brackets, in all sections. A question mark (?) indicates date not verified.

Abarr, [*Ab'-ahr*], Yuma. (E 1921) Founded by Dr. D. C. Brown and at that time called Brownsville. In 1923 S. E. Hoffman started a store and had the town site surveyed, platted, and recorded. When a post office was opened, because there was another Colorado town named Brownsville, the name was changed to Abarr. The name was Hoffman's wife's maiden name. Hoffman was the first postmaster.

Adams City, Adams. (E 1923) For the county, which in turn, for Gov. Alva Adams. Although platted about 1901, it was not until a post office was established in 1923 that formal recognition was made. Not shown on the state highway map, its location is about six miles north of Denver on U.S. 85; map quadrants about E-F 17.

Agate, Elbert. (E 1876?) While the origin of the name is unverified, it is believed the Union Pacific Railroad selected the name. One authority states the name reflects agate (rock) specimens found in the area, and for Indian arrowheads made of the same variety of chalcedony quartz. One version is that there was a large gate on the townsite through which travelers passed. Gradually the words were fused in pronunciation and written as one: A Gate to Agate. An earlier name was Gebhard.

Aguilar, [*Ag'-ih-lar*], Las Animas. (E 1867; I 1894; P 699) First a trading post for Indians and Spanish-American farmers, the town was founded by Agapita Rivali. When the town sought incorporation it was named for Jose Ramon Aguilar, prominent pioneer of southern Colorado.

Akron, Washington. (E 1882; I 1887; P 1,775) County seat. Named by a Mrs. Calvert, wife of a railroad official, for her home town, Akron, Ohio. The name is Greek, meaning "summit," and is considered appropriate because Akron is on the highest point on the Chicago, Burlington & Quincy Railroad in Colorado. (Elev. 6,400 ft.)

Alamosa, [*Al-uh-moh'suh*],Alamosa. (E 1878; I 1878; P 6,985) County seat. Founded by ex-Gov. A. C. Hunt, president of the Denver & Rio Grande Construction Co. He named the town Alamosa, Spanish for "cottonwood grove." An earlier settlement on the site, Wayside, a stage coach stop (1876), was abandoned before the platting of the present town.

Allenspark, Boulder. (E 1870?) For an early settler, Alonzo Allen, who homesteaded in 1859. The first post office, built in the 1870's, was desroyed by fire in 1894. A later one was built two miles from the original site.

Allison, La Plata. (E 1901) First called Vallejo, it was changed by postal authorities because of confusion with a California town. The new name was selected by the residents to honor Allison Stocker, a pioneer contractor and builder of many Denver buildings, and prominent in the development of this area of La Plata County.

Alma, Park. (E 1872; I 1873; P 73) Three versions exist. That it was named for Alma James, wife of a Fairplay merchant who opened the first store there; that it was named for Alma Graves, wife of Abner Graves, who operated the Alma Mine; that it was named for Alma Jaynes, popular daughter of an early settler.

Almont {*Al'mahnt*], Gunnison. (E 1881) Samual Fisher, an early and prominent Gunnison County rancher, purchased a fine stallion, son of the famous Almont of Kentucky. When the Denver & Rio Grande Railroad built to Fisher's ranch and a town grew up there in 1881, the settlement was named for the great race horse that had sired Fisher's stallion.

Amherst [*Am'erst*], Phillips. (E 1887 ?) Supposedly named by an early rancher from Amherst, Mass., who settled in Colorado. Many communities were named by early residents for their former "back east" towns; sometimes inspired by home-sickness.

Antero Junction, Park. (E 1892 ?) For Uintah Ute Chief Antero, at the junction of U.S. 285 and 24. The building of nearby Antero Reservoir began in 1892 and the original road from Hartsel passed on the south side of the reservoir. No community as such exists. An Antero was, earlier, shown on maps, including the Colorado Midland Railway. A post office is shown in records for a short period, but it is not known if it ever operated. Chief Antero was among the chiefs who, in 1873, signed a treaty ceding rich mineral lands in the San Juan district to the U.S.

Anton, Washington. (E 1920?) Maurice S. Walters, familiar with Canton, Neb., before homesteading in Colorado, turned in the name Canton when suggestions were asked for naming a new post office and store. His suggestion was misread—as Anton. The name remained. (While there is some doubt about this version, nothing has been shown to refute it.)

Antonito [*An-tuh-nee'toh*], Conejos. (E 1881; I 1889; P 1,113) Founded by the Denver & Rio Grande Railroad, for the San Antonio Mountains and San Antonio River in the vicinity. The name is Spanish, meaning "little Anthony."

Arapahoe [*Uh-rap'-uh-hoh*], Cheyenne. (E 1870) Named for the Arapaho Indians who lived in this region. Their own name for themselves was Inunaina, "our people." The two versions of spelling the place name (with and without the "e") are interchangeable, but "Arapaho" appears on Goverment maps and data. A post office was established in 1860 while Arapahoe was in Kansas Territory, but existed less than two years.

Arboles [*Are'-bowl-las*], Archuleta. (E 1881) Spanish name for "trees," and refers to the wooded growth along the banks of the nearby Piedra River.

Arlington, Kiowa. (E 1887) Founded as Juliet, its present name was given by the Missouri Pacific Railroad, and honors one of its officials.

Aroya [*Uh-roy' -yuh*], Cheyenne. (E 1872) Named for a deep gulch that runs through the town. The word is a corruption of the Spanish word "arroyo," meaning "rivulet," and applied in the New World to the courses cut by intermittent streams in flood time. Aroya is built on the site of the ranch owned by T.C. Schilling, one of the founders of the Schilling Tea Co.

Arriba [*Arr'-ib-a*], Lincoln. (E 1898; I 1918; P 254) A Spanish word meaning "above" or "over" and referring to the town's altitude (5,239 ft.) compared with others in the region.

Arriola [*Air-ee-oh'-luh*], Montezuma. (E 1885 ?) For an early Spanish military man, but no details are recorded. Early known as one of the choice locations in Montezuma Valley.

Arvada [*Ahr-vad'-uh*], Adams and Jefferson. (E 1880; I 1904; P 46,814) Named for Hiram Arvada Hoskin, brother-in-law of the wife of the founder, B. F. Wadsworth. In earlier days (1860) it was known as Ralston Point and Ralston Station for the creek where early placer miners first discovered "color" in their gold pans. (Wadsworth Boulevard is a major north-south thoroughfare in the city.)

Aspen, Pitkin. (E 1880; I 1881; P 2,404) County seat. Townsite surveyor, B. Clark Wheeler, named the town for the profuse growth of aspen trees in the vicinity. Formerly (1879) it was known as Ute City.

Atwood, Logan. (E 1885) Victor Wilson brought a colony from Abiline, Kan. A Unitarian, Wilson named the town for a minister of that sect, the Rev. John S. Atwood of Boston, Mass.

Ault, Weld. (E 1888; I 1904; P 841) For Alexander Ault, pioneer miller of Fort Collins. Ault purchased the entire crop raised in the area for many years before grain storage facilities were available in the vicinity. For this service to the community the town adopted his name when a post office was established in 1904.

Aurora, Adams and Arapahoe. (E 1891; I 1903; P 74,974) First named Fletcher, for Donald Fletcher, one of the town promoters. The name was changed to its present one upon incorporation because town officials thought the new name "classier." The name is a Latin word meaning "dawn" or "morning." (When Adams County was formed from Arapahoe County in 1902, the new county line divided the main street in Aurora. Residents south of E. Colfax Ave. pay taxes in Littleton; those north of Colfax pay taxes in Brighton.)

Austin [*Aws'-tin*], Delta. (E 1900; P 1,163) Named for Austin Miller, rancher and land-owner, who gave the Denver & Rio Grande Railroad land for its right of way and the townsite. Post office established in 1905.

Avon, Eagle. (E 1884) Thought to have been named by an Englishman for England's Avon River. First title to the land was given to William L. Swift. However, when it was listed as a railroad station in 1889, it was spelled Avin, and later changed to its present spelling.

Avondale [*Av'-on-dale*], Pueblo. (E 1890 ?) An Englishman, Sam Taylor, one of the pioneer settlers, named it for his old home, Stratford-on-Avon, England. Earlier it was known as Forest Park. Taylor started the Taylor Mercantile Co. in 1894; changed to Arapahoe Super Market in 1952.

Bailey [*Bay'-lee*], Park. (E 1864) Named for a settler, William Bailey, who established a hotel and stage station in 1864. Known as Bailey's Ranch, the station's name was shortened and used by the settlement. In 1878, the narrow-gauge Denver & South Park Railroad made Bailey its terminal. Bailey's wife was the sister of the famous "snow-shoe itinerant," the Rev. John Dyer.

Barnesville, Weld. (E 1908) For the family name of Charles and George Barnes. The brothers platted a town, hoping it would grow to a large size, when the railroad came to the area—a spur track from a Greeley to Briggsdale line.

Bartlett, Baca. (E 1928) When the Santa Fe Railway built a branch line through here in 1928, to the town of Pritchett, the section point was named for an official of the railroad.

Basalt [*Ba-salt'*], Eagle and Pitkin. (E 1882; I 1901; P 419) Founded when the Colorado Midland Railroad was built through here and used as a division point. Named for Basalt Peak (10,800 ft.), which rises from the center of a large outcrop of basaltic lava.

Baxter, Pueblo. (E 1859 ?) Named for Oliver H.P. Baxter, a Colorado pioneer of 1859, who took up the land upon which the settlement was founded.

Bayfield, La Plata. (E 1886; I 1906; P 320) The town was laid out by

W.A.Bay, for whom it was named. The post office was formerly Los Pinos.

Bedrock, Montrose. (E 1883) Probably because the post office is built on a bedrock of sandstone. A general store which housed the post office was constructed in 1883.

Bellvue, Larimer. (E 1882) A combination of the French words "belle" meaning beautiful, and "vue," meaning view, by founder Jacob Fowler in 1882. Pioneer Fowler was one of the first to show fruit could successfully be grown in Colorado.

Bennett, Adams. (E 1870; I 1930; P 613) For H.P. Bennett, an early-day Denver postmaster. First called Kiowa, for nearby Kiowa Creek. Kiowa is an Indian tribe name.

Bergen Park, Jefferson. (E 1859) For Thomas C. Bergen, one of the earliest settlers west of Denver. He managed a hotel and stage station and the area assumed his name. Not shown on the state highway map it is at the junction of State Highways 74 and 103; map quadrants F-15.

Berthoud [*Berth'-ud*], Larimer. (E 1877; I 1888; P 1,446) Named for Capt. Edward L. Berthoud, chief civil engineer of the Colorado Central Railroad when the line reached here. Berthoud was also the discoverer of Berthoud Pass. Settlement earlier was known as "Little Thompson," with a post office opening in the spring of 1875.

Berts Corner, Larimer. (E 1935 ?) For Bert Foote, who operated a filling station and had tourist cabins there in the 1930s. It is possible a gas station and store occupied the site prior to Foote, but verification has not been made. A long, sweeping curve on the highway (287) into Berthoud was constructed in 1936.

Beshoar Jct. [*Besh'-or*], Las Animas. (E 1888 ?) For Michael Beshoar, pioneer physician, who was an early and colorful settler of Trinidad, Colo. A true community never existed, though a post office was established for a short time (1901-03).

Bethune [*Beth-yoon'*], Kit Carson. (E 1918; I 1926; P 99) Founded during World War I, it was named for a town in France. Possibly, it is thought, because some of the area men sent overseas went to that part of France.

Beulah [*Byoo'-lah*], Pueblo. (E 1862) First known as Mace's Hole, because a Mexican outlaw, Juan Mace, once made the valley his hiding place. Later, a Reverend Gaylord settled and, feeling the name lacked beauty, suggested the present name. A vote was taken at a social gathering and Beulah, a Hebraic word meaning "married' or "inhabited," won by two votes over the name Silver Glen. At one time the town was also known as Devil's Hole.

Black Forest, El Paso. (E 1866 ?) For the huge stands of ponderosa pine trees covering thousands of acres, and which sparked an early timber industry in the 1870s.

Black Hawk, Gilpin. (E 1859; I 1864; P 217) From an early mining company which brought into the area a quartz mill bearing as a trademark the name of the famous Indian chief, Black Hawk. The name seems to be spelled as one word—Blackhawk—as often as two. The latter, however, is the present official spelling.

Blakeland, Arapahoe. (E 1919 ?) Named by Mrs. Mary N. Blake as a coined word; possibly when she operated the Blakeland Poultry Farms. Later, at the Blakeland junction (there was never a settlement), she had a restaurant known as the Coffee Pot, which suffered a major fire in 1931.

Blanca [*Blang'-kuh*], Costilla. (E 1908; I 1910; P 212) The town was born of a land lottery, when people in all parts of the country were sold small tracts with the understanding they would be eligible for larger plots of ground. Town named for its location at foot of Mount Blanca (14,363 ft.), Spanish for "white."

Blue Mountain, Moffat. (P.O. E 1950) For the east-west Blue Mountain Range, on whose north side is Dinosaur National Monument. The post office was moved here from Skull Creek, where it had been established in 1929.

Blue River, Summit (E 1964; I 1964; P 8) For the clear blue-colored stream, one of the early Colorado waters which attracted placer mining in the gold rush days. Many "towns" came and went along this and other important gold-country rivers.

Bonanza, Saguache. (E 1880; I 1881; P 10) "Boys, she's a bonanza," said one of the early prospectors whose discoveries helped settle the region. The name clung to the town that grew up on the site of this strike. Bonanza is a Spanish word meaning "prosperity," and was often used for a rich body of ore. Only a few valuable claims were found in the Bonanza area, however, and the population—once up to 1,300—drifted away after 1882.

Boncarbo, Las Animas. (E 1915) Sometimes spelled Bon Carbo, the name is a corruption of "bon carbon," French for "good coal." It was given by Abe Thompson, an official of the American Smelting & Refining Co. about 1915. A post office was established in 1917. Much of the coal mined here was sent to Cokedale for coking.

Bond, Eagle. (E 1934) On June 16, 1934, a celebration was held here (0.7 mile west of Orestod) at the Dotsero Cutoff—from the Denver & Rio Grande Western Railroad main line at Dotsero to the Denver & Salt Lake Railroad at Orestod. The connection shortened the rail distance between Denver and Salt Lake City by 173 miles. The community took its name from the connection—or bond—of the cutoff rails. Orestod is the name Dotsero spelled backwards. (See also: Dotsero.)

Boone, Pueblo. (E 1860, I 1956; P 448) Named by Col. A. G. Boone, great-grandson of Kentucky pioneer, Daniel Boone. Earlier it was known as Booneville and Boon Town. Colonel Boone was a postmaster here for several years, and was an early Indian Agent.

Boulder, Boulder. (E 1859; I 1871; P 66,870) County seat. Gold seekers came here in the fall of 1858; the settlement was the outgrowth of mining activity in the mountains to the west. The name comes from the profusion of boulders in the vicinity.

Bow Mar [*Bo'-Mar*], Arapahoe-Jefferson. (E 1958; I 1958; P 945) Located between Bowles and Marston lakes, the name reflects the combination of the first syllables from each of the lakes. Bow Mar, too, has a small lake.

Bowie [*Boh'-ee*], Delta. (E 1907) Formerly a coal camp called Reading, but changed when a post office was established. The name honored Alexander Bowie, native of Scotland, who operated coal mines in the east and west. In 1906 he helped develop the Juanita Coal & Coke Co. at Reading, and became part owner and general manager. After his death in 1917 the mine was operated by his four sons. Through the 1950's to the early 1970's the company was managed by a grandson. In 1974 JCCC was sold to Adolph Coors Co., Golden.

Boyero [*Boy-yer'-oh*], Lincoln. (E 1870) Spanish, meaning "cow herd" or "ox-driver." According to a local story, the name was used here as "bull pen," given the settlement by Mexican laborers because of the stockyards. A town plat was filed in 1908, on part of the land of the first homesteader, Dr. C.A. Kelsey.

Brandon [*Bran'-duhn*], Kiowa. (E 1887 ?) While the origin is unknown, the post office was probably named for a nearby reservoir, Lake Brandon. (For the naming of several towns in the area, see: Haswell, Colo.)

Branson [*Bran'-suhn*], Las Animas. (E 1916; I 1921; P 70) The town was named for Al Branson of Trinidad, who was active in founding the settlement. At various times it was known as Wilson, Wilson Switch, and Coloflats. As Coloflats, a post office was established in 1915.

Breckenridge, Summit. (E 1859; I 1880; P 548) County seat. Founded by a party of prospectors under Gen. George E. Spencer, who, after the Civil War, was a U. S. Senator from Alabama. The town was named in honor of John Cabell Breckinridge, then United States Vice President. The flattering gesture was intended to prompt Congress to create a post office for the new settlement. It did. Because of Breckinridge's sympathy for the Confederacy, the citizens—ardent Unionists—petitioned Congress to change the name of the town. Accordingly, the first "i" was changed to "e," the spelling of the present form.

Breen, La Plata. (E 1900) Named for Dr. Thomas Breen, superintendent of the Fort Lewis Indian School in 1900.

Briggsdale, Weld. (E 1909) For Frank M. Briggs, a farmer and real estate dealer, who helped plat the townsite.

Brighton, Adams. (E 1882; I 1887; P 8,309) County seat. Named for Brighton, Mass., home town of Mrs. D.F. Carmichael, wife of the man who laid out the town. Originally it was known as Hughes Junction, for Gen. Bela M. Hughes, who came to Colorado in 1861 as president of the Overland Mail Co.

Bristol, Prowers. (E 1906) For C.H. Bristol, an official of the Santa Fe Railway, also owner of land in the vicinity. Supposedly Bristol's name was to have been given to the unincorporated town of Lancaster (now Hartman). Because of an error of some kind the names were given to the "wrong towns." The mistake was never corrected. (See: Hartman, Colo.)

Broadmoor [*Broad'-more*], El Paso. (E 1890) For the sweeping terrain of the area and named by the Broadmoor Land & Investment Co. headed by Count James Pourtales who, in 1891, opened a casino in the tract. Spencer Penrose's new Broadmoor Hotel formally opened on the same site in 1918.

Broomfield, Adams-Boulder-Jefferson. (E 1887; I 1961; P 7,261) Originally known as Zang's Spur, for Philip Zang, Denver business man and brewer, who bred Percheron horses nearby. When the Denver & Salt Lake Railway narrow-gauge established a station here, the present name was adopted. Railroad officials noticed a small field of broom corn nearby and suggested the name Broomfield.

Brush, Morgan. (E 1882; I 1884; P 3,377) For a pioneer cattleman of the South Platte Valley, Jared L. Brush. Long before the town was established the site was a favorite shipping point on the old Texas-Montana cattle trail, and was known among cattlemen as Beaver Creek.

Buckingham, Weld. (E 1888) For C.D. Buckingham, superintendent of the McCook division of the Burlington Railroad. Buckingham also surveyed and platted the townsite.

Buena Vista [*Byoo'-nuh vihs-tuh*], Chaffee. (E 1879; I 1879; P 1,962) A Spanish name meaning "good view." No record of who first applied the term here.

Buffalo Creek, Jefferson. (E 1877 ?) For a stream of the same name. Fire destroyed the town three times. It was also known as Buffalo. Whether the small waterway was named for the bison's common name, or another city (such as Buffalo, N.Y.) is not known.

Buford [*Bue'-ford*], Rio Blanco. (E 1890)Named for a "Colonel Buford" who served as a guide for Theodore Roosevelt when he was in the area on a hunting trip.

Burlington, Kit Carson. (E 1887; I 1888; P 2,828) County seat. The first settlement here, in 1886, was platted and named Lowell. The plat was abandoned and a new one covering the same land was filed. The original town was moved to the site in 1887, and called Burlington. The name is said to have been selected because many of the residents came from Burlington, Kan.

Burns, Eagle. (E 1895) Named for Jack Burns, an early trapper, who built his cabin here. He died in 1891. The date shown for establishment is when the post office was granted. It is likely a community was functioning earlier, but no data is available.

Byers [*Bigh'-ers*], Arapahoe. (E 1868) Founded by a scout named Oliver P. Wiggins, it was first called Bijou. It was renamed for William N. Byers, founder, and publisher of the state's oldest newspaper, the *Rocky Mountain News*, Denver, founded in 1859. (See: Deer Trail and Wiggins.)

Caddoa [*Cad'-doe*], Bent. (E 1863) Several versions exist for this town name at the site of Martin Reservoir. Most likely is that it was named for the Caddoan linguistic stock, to which the Pawnee, Caddo proper, and Wichita tribes belong. Other versions also link it to the Caddo Indians.

Cahone [*Ca-hoe-n'-ee*], Dolores. (E 1912 ?) From the Spanish word "cajon," meaning "little box." Named by the first postmaster, Bert Ballenger, for a nearby box-like canyon.

Calhan [*Kal'-un*], El Paso. (E 1888; I 1919; P 465) Founded as a railroad water-tank station because good water was available at shallow depth from Big Sandy Creek. Named, originally, Calahan for a contractor who built this section of the Chicago, Rock Island & Pacific Railroad. The railroad, in listing on its time tables, shorted the name to Calhan, its present form.

Cameo, Mesa. (E 1907) For the outline of a stone formation on the face of a cliff overlooking the settlement. John McNeil, president of the Grand Junction Fuel & Mining Co., opened the Cameo Coal Mine and founded the town.

Camp Bird, Ouray. (E 1896) Named for the famous Camp Bird Gold Mine. Originally a silver claim, the mine which made Thomas J. Walsh a millionaire, produced almost $4 million in six years (between 1896 and 1902). The mine was named for the camp bird, the miners' name for the Rocky Mountain or Canada Jay; also called the "Whiskey Jack." (See: Ouray, Colo.)

Campion, Larimer. (E 1907) For John E. Campion, an engineer and surveyor with the Colorado Central Railroad. The town was settled by members of the Seventh Day Adventists, who started the Campion Academy, a co-educational boarding school.

Campo, Baca. (E 1912; I 1950; P 206) For the Spanish word campo, meaning "field."

Canon City [*Can'-yun City*], Fremont. (E 1859; I 1872; P 11,011) County seat. Name derived from its site being near the Grand Canyon of the Arkansas River. The site was a camping ground for Zebulon Pike in 1806. City is location of the Colorado State Penitentiary.

Capulin [*Cap-you'-lin*], Conejos. (E 1867) Founded by Spanish immigrants from Caliente, N.M., the name is a Spanish word meaning "choke-cherry."

Carbondale, Garfield. (E 1883; I 1888; P 726) Named by John Mankin, one of the town founders, for his home town in Pennsylvania.

Carlton, Prowers. (E 1886) Early listed as Conroe and Grote, the town site was platted by C.H. (Judge) Frybarger of the Colorado Land & Title Co. No suggestion why the name Carlton was chosen. It's possible it honored a firm member or railroad executive.

Carr, Weld. (E 1872 ?) For Robert E. Carr, associated with former Territorial Gov. John Evans, who completed this section of the Union Pacific Railroad. Carr later became president of the Kansas-Pacific Railroad.

Cascade, El Paso. (E 1886) For the many beautiful waterfalls in the surrounding canyon streams. Settlers were Kansans, most of whom were associated with the Santa Fe Railway. In 1889 the Pikes Peak carriage road was built from this point. The road (improved) still exists as a toll road to the top of the 14,110 ft. mountain.

Castle Rock, Douglas. (E 1874; I 1881; P 1,531) County seat. For the nearby castellated rock formation. The famous landmark was named by Dr. Edwin James, botanist of Maj. Stephen Long's expedition of 1820.

Cedaredge, Delta. (E 1882; I 1907; P 581) One version: For the heavy belt of cedar trees at the nearby edge of Grand Mesa; another is that the town grew on the site of "Cedar edge," the ranch of Henry Kohler, and that the name was later compounded into a single word.

Cedarwood, Pueblo. (E 1912) Founded as a station on the Colorado & Southern Railroad and named by the Rev. J.H. White, a nearby settler, for the cedar trees in the area. It was once two words: Cedar Wood.

Center, Rio Grande and Saguache. (E 1898; I 1907; P 1,470) Founded and platted by J.L. Hunt, owner of the townsite land, and originally called Centerview. Later it was renamed by the post office department. Presumably the name is because the town is in the central part of the San Luis Valley.

Central City, Gilpin. (E 1859; I 1864; P 228) County seat. Begun as a trading center for miners in surrounding communities, *Rocky Mountain News* publisher, William N. Byers, suggested the name because of the town's hub location among the gold camps. It reached a peak population of about 10,000. The first legal execution under Colorado Territorial government took place here in January, 1864, when a man named Van Horn was hanged for murder.

Chama [*Chah'-muh*], Costilla. (E 1860) Founded by a party of men from Chamita, N.M., on the bank of the Culebra River. The name is Spanish for "lass" or "little girl," and was named for the settlers' former home. While the first settlers were driven off by Indians, a later settlement retained the same name. (Note: There is a Chama, New Mexico, as well; about 8 miles south of the Colorado-New Mexico border after crossing Cumbres Pass.)

Cheney Center [*Chee'-nee*], Prowers. (E 1886 ?) For Cheney Center, Kan., which suggests the first settlers came from that town. The Kansas community, in turn, was named for B.P. Cheney, a stockholder of the Atchison, Topeka & Santa Fe Railway. It was also called Wilson Junction.

Cheraw [*Chair-aw'*], Otero. (E 1907; I 1917; P 129) Named for a nearby lake, which, it is thought, derived its name from the Cheraw Indian tribe; member of the Siouan family and originally in Virginia and the Carolinas.

Cherry Hills Village, Arapahoe. (E 1870; I 1945; P 4,605) For the large cherry orchards which were once in the area. The trees are long gone, replaced by an area of fine homes and estates.

Cheyenne Wells, Cheyenne. (E 1870; I 1890; P 982) County seat. A station on the Union Pacific Railroad. The name comes from several wells that were dug at the old town site, coupled with the name of the Indian tribe then inhabiting the area. Cheyenne Wells was the name of a stage station five miles north of the present town on the old Smokey Hill Stage Route.

Chimney Rock, Archuleta. (E 1880 ?) The Spanish term "piedra parada" translates to Chimney Rock, for a local landmark. On early maps the name is Piedre. Prior to the present name it was Dyke. This, a variant of dike, is also Spanish for a rock outcropping.

Chipita Park [*Chip-eet'-uh*], El Paso. (E 1890) Named for Chipeta, wife of Ute Indian Chief Ouray. First known as Ute Park but renamed in 1927 when it was sold to the Frank Mancrofts. Oddly, the official spelling of the community differs from the actual spelling of Chipeta. (See: Ouray, Colo.)

Chivington [*Shiv'-ing-ton*], Kiowa. (E 1887) Named for Col. John M. Chivington, a former minister, whose volunteer troops in 1864 engaged in a bloody battle with Indians at Sand Creek, near the town's location. (The fight has generated much controversy and is often referred to as the "Sand Creek massacre.")

Chromo [*Kroh'-moh*], Archuleta. (E 1881) Originally known as Price, for its first postmaster, Charles W. Price, 1881. The post office was discontinued and mail received at Durango. When application was later made for a new post office authorities advised a new name to avoid confusion with Price, Utah. Price is said to have suggested Chromo, as he had seen and named Chromo Mountain, N.M.,many years before. The name is a Greek word for "color," suitable for the vivid landscape in the vicinity.

Cimarron [*Sim-uh-rohn'*], Montrose. (E 1875 ?) From the Cimarron River on which it is located. The name is Spanish, meaning "wild" or "unruly." An 1862 issue of Harper's Magazine noted the word Cimarron was the Mexican appellation for the Rocky Mountain or Big Horn sheep.

Clark, Routt. (POE 1889) For a resident named Clark, but which one is uncertain. Possibly for Worthington Clark, a stagecoacher of Walden, Colo. Possibly for Rufus Clark who may have been the first postmaster. "Postmaster Clark" and his wife, Emily, are said to be buried in the Clark Cemetery. The community was in a placer mining area and remained small. A one-room school is still used, on occasion, for community functions.

Clarkville, Yuma. (E 1933) Platted by Louis Nielsen, and named for Ted Clark, who was appointed the first postmaster in 1936. It is called the "baby of Yuma County's ghost towns." While there is still a lively community group in the area, it is not the thriving, prosperous center it was until the early 1970's.

Clifton, Mesa. (E 1882) Because of the Book Cliffs near the Denver & Rio Grande Railroad at this point. Originally applied to a section of track and later for a station; later the town grew and adopted the name.

Climax, Lake. (E 1917) Alternately called Fremont Pass and Climax, the latter because it was the highest point on the D&RGW Railroad. The name became official when a post office was established. Fremont—explorer John C.—has his name honored by Fremont Pass, near Climax. Climax produces a large part of the world's supply of molybdenum, a steel hardener.

Coal Creek, Fremont. (E 1872; I 1882; P 225) Taken from that of a nearby stream, so-called because of the seams of coal along its sides.

Coaldale, Fremont. (E 1884) From a coal mining camp which started the site. Earlier called De Pauls. Later the town became the center of gypsum mining, there being large deposits of this element in the area.

Coalmont, Jackson. (E 1911) From a contraction of "coal mountain," because of the coal deposits in the area. The coal is so close to the surface that it was early a strip-mining operation.

Cokedale, Las Animas. (E 1906; I 1948; P 101) A station on the Denver & Rio Grande Western Railroad and a coal mining community, plus ovens to make coke.

Collbran [*Coal'-bran*], Mesa. (E 1891; I 1908; P 225) Originally named Hawhurst but through the influence of Dr. deBeque (founder of De Beque) it was changed to Collbran, a former railroad man of the community.

Colorado City, Pueblo. (E 1963) A generic name reflecting a new city in the state, and named by the Colorado City Development Co. The community is planned for an eventual population of 30,000. The site was formerly Crow Junction, which, in the 1880's, boasted a post office. (The name should not be confused with an earlier Colorado City near Colorado Springs.)

Colorado Springs, El Paso. (E 1871; I 1886; P 135,060) County seat. Laid out near the site of the older settlement of Colorado City, it takes its name from the numerous mineral springs in the area. For a time it was known as El Paso (Spanish: "the pass") because of its proximity to Ute Pass. Gen. William J. Palmer, head of the Denver & Rio Grande Western Railroad, was the moving force in the Colorado Springs Co. which organized the city.

Columbine, Routt. (E 1895) For the Colorado state flower, which grew here in profusion.

Columbine Valley, Arapahoe. (E 1959; I 1959; P 481) A community named after the nearby Columbine Country Club which had been established some time earlier. It, in turn, is thought to have taken the name from the official state flower.

Commerce City, Adams. (E 1952; I 1952; P 17,407) Formerly Commerce Town, a community predominantly industrial from its early beginnings in the early 1900's.

Como [*Coe'-moe*], Park. (E 1879) Originally the "Stubbs Ranch," it was mainly occupied by Italian coal miners. The name was taken from Lake Como in Italy; probably a long-distance case of home-sickness.

Conejos [*Con'-aye-ohs*], Conejos. (E 1855) County seat. One of the oldest towns in the state, with the first church and first convent built in Colorado. The name Conejos is the Spanish word for "rabbit."

Conifer, Jefferson. (E 1860) For the thick growth of conifers in the area. First known as Hutchison, for early settler George Hutchison. Later it was known as Junction City, changing to the present name in 1900. A landmark well on Rte. 73, in the center of the road, was known as Hutchison-Bradford Junction.

Cope [*Kohp*], Washington. (E 1888) Named for its founder, Johnathan C. Cope, an employee of the Burlington Railroad. Cope was sent to take a homestead that would serve as a rail terminal for a projected line. The settlement grew around his ranch house. However, the post office was first known as Gray.

Cornish, Weld. (E 1911) For a Mr. Cornish, a civil engineer of the Union Pacific Railroad. The site was laid out by Henry Breder, owner of the land, when the railroad built a branch through the area, from Greeley to Briggsdale.

Cortez, Montezuma. (E 1886; I 1902; P 6,032) County seat. For a Spanish leader who conquered Mexico in the 16th century. Name suggested by James W. Hanna , homesteader, who sold the site to the Montezuma Land & Development Co.

Cotopaxi [*Coat-oh-pax'-ee*], Fremont. (E 1873 ?) Two versions exist for the name. One is that it is of Quicha Indian origin, meaning "shining pile;" the other as meaning "low pass." It is thought the name came from the Cotopaxi Volcano in South America. A hill south of the town bears the same name, possibly given by Spanish explorers.

Cowdrey [*Kou'-dree*], Jackson. (E 1882) For an early settler, Charles Cowdrey, who established a hotel or roadhouse in the village.

Craig, Moffat. (E 1889; I 1908; P 4,205) County seat. From the name of the promoter, the Rev. Bayard Craig, who laid out the site for his Craig Townsite Co. Settlement began earlier when ranch claims were developed.

Crawford, Delta. (E 1882; I 1910; P 171) Named for George A. Crawford, frontier capitalist, speculator, and former governor of Kansas, who started many towns on Colorado's western slope in the 1880's.

Creede [*Creed*], Mineral. (E 1890; I 1892; P 653) County seat. Nicholas C. Creede, shortly after the founding, made important mineral discoveries and almost overnight the influx of miners and others swelled the population to 10,000. Creede absorbed several camps in its rapid growth including Amethyst, Jimtown, and Bachelor. Jesse James' killer, Bob Ford, met his end here, and poet Cy Warman immortalized the town with the lines "It's day all day in the daytime, and there is no night in Creede."

Crested Butte, Gunnison. (E 1879; I 1880; P 372) For a nearby mountain whose top resembles a cock's comb. The town was founded by Howard F. Smith who brought the first saw mill here.

Crestone [*Kres-tohn'*], Saguache. (E 1879; I 1902; P 34) Founded by gold prospectors, the name comes from nearby Crestone Peak (14,291 ft.). The word is Spanish for "cock's comb," (a free translation).

Cripple Creek, Teller. (E 1891; I 1892; P 425) County seat. From a stream, Cripple Creek, named by early cowboys because a cow was crippled attempting to cross it. The site was first homesteaded in 1876 by William W. Womack of Kentucky. Later, "Bob" Womack, son of the original owner prospected for gold. His assays of ore brought many miners to the area and a mining camp known as Fremont soon mushroomed. The name was changed to its present one after a town was platted, and is known as one of the great gold camps of the early West.

Crook, Logan. (E 1881; I 1918; P 199) Named by the Union Pacific Railroad after Maj. Gen. George R. Crook. He commanded the Dept. of the Platte from 1875 to 1882. It was Crook who captured the outlaw Apache Indian, Geronimo.

Crowley [*Krow'-lee*], Crowley. (E 1880; I 1921; P 216) For John H. Crowley, State Senator from Otero County in 1911, when Crowley County was organized from a portion of Otero.

Cuchara [*Coo-chair'-uh*], Huerfano. (E 1916) Spanish word meaning "spoon." Named for the Cuchara River which, in turn, derived its name from the spoon-like-shape of the valley through which it flows. A post office at Cuchara Camps was moved to the present site in 1957. Another, earlier Cucharas, northeast of Walsenburg (and sometimes spelled Cacharas), also on the river, was prominent in the early 1870's.

Dacono [*Day-co'-no*], Weld. (E 1906; I 1908; P 360) First established as a coal mine by C.L. Baum. As production increased a settlement grew around the mine. Baum named the village Dacono, a word coined from the first two letters of his wife's name, Daisy, and from the corresponding letters of the names of two of her friends, Cora Van Voorhies and Nona Brooks. Along with Firestone and Frederick, it is one of the "tri-cities."

Dailey, Logan. (E 1914) When in June, 1914, the Burlington Railroad put up a siding on the site of the town, it gave the name Dailey, for James Dailey, trainmaster, who came from Lincoln, Neb.

DeBeque [*Di-bek'*], Mesa. (E 1889; I 1890; P 155) For Dr. Wallace A. E. deBeque, who settled in the locality in 1883, coming from Fairplay, Colo., where he was a physician. In 1887 his family moved to the site of the present town and the new post office was named DeBeque in 1888. The Curtis Town & Land Co. laid out the townsite in 1889. (See: Collbran.)

Deckers, Douglas. (E 1885 ?) Formerly known as Daffodil, and later Pemberton. Name changed in 1912 to Deckers. Steve Decker in earlier days had a general store and saloon in the South Platte River community. It has always been a summer fishing resort.

Deer Ridge, Larimer. (E 1913) A ridge in Rocky Mountain National Park leading to Deer Mountain (9,937 ft.) In 1913 the Estes Park Women's Club raised funds to pay for a trail to the top of Deer Mountain. This followed the ridge. The date, therefore, is arbitrary.

Deer Trail, Arapahoe. (E 1870; I 1920; P 374) Founded and named by frontiersman Oliver P. Wiggins, for the place where deer drank from Bijou Creek. (See: Byers and Wiggins, Colo.)

Del Norte [*Del Nort'*], Rio Grande. (E 1872; I 1885; P 1,569) County seat. Founded and named by a group of ambitious gold seekers. The name is from the Rio Grande del Norte, Spanish for "great river of the north," the present Rio Grande that flows through the town.

Delhi [*Del'-hie*], Las Animas. (E 1899 ?) Possibly for the city in India, which was often applied to U.S. communities as an exotic name without other reason. Once called Edwest for a resident of that name. Post office changes to and from Delhi include Bloom (formerly named Iron Spring) as well as Edwest.

Delta, Delta. (E 1882; I 1882; P 3,694) County seat. From its location on the delta at the mouth of the Uncompahgre River. Formerly known as Uncompahgre, for the nearby river, mountain range, and plateau.

Denver, Denver. (E 1858; I 1861; P 514,678) County seat, state capitol. Only combined city and county in state. First real settlement came with discovery of placer gold. Auraria, named by prospectors from Auraria, Ga., was formed on west side of Cherry Creek. Another party, headed by Gen. William Larimer of Leavenworth, Kan., settled on the opposite side of the stream and formed the Denver City Co. Their settlement was named for James W. Denver, Governor of Kansas Territory. Rivalry between the two towns continued until April, 1860, when they consolidated into one municipality, Denver.

Deora [*Dee-oh'-ruh*], Baca. (E 1920) From two Spanish words, "de" and "oro," meaning "of gold." Suggested by Postmistress Ethel Falk when post office was established May 20, 1920.

Devine, Pueblo. (E 1876 ?) Both origin and date are uncertain. The local belief is that it honors Thomas Devine, assistant secretary of the Missouri Pacific Railway in 1902. Missouri Pacific records do not show this but indicate Devine, Tex., was named for the official who was also a prominent Texas jurist. The line from Kansas to Pueblo was completed in 1887. The Santa Fe Railway's line, also going through Devine, was opened in 1876. Devine first was named Vineland. Because it was confused with nearby Vineland (still in existence) it was changed. One thought is that it could be still honoring "the vines" as originally.

Dillon [*Dil'-uhn*] , Summit. (E 1880; I 1883; P 182) For gold seeker Tom Dillon, who became lost, and when he appeared at Golden described his wanderings to include a wide valley where three rivers met. Later explorers found the area and named it in his honor. Since 1961, the town is a mile north of its original site. Dillon was moved in its entirety when Dillon Reservoir was built, covering the old location—and many more square miles.

Dinosaur, Moffat. (E 1914; I 1947; P 247) Early known as Artesia, for a New Mexico town of the same name and for its own artesian wells. In 1965 the name was changed to aid tourism with its proximity to Dinosaur National Monument, whose headquarters are here. When the name was changed, so were the street names; all now called by various dinosaur names.

Divide, Teller. (E 1877) For its location on the divide of the Front Range, highest point on the route of US 24 between the drainage basins of Fountain Creek and the South Platte River. It was the terminal of a toll road into the Cripple Creek mining district.

Dolores [*Duh-loh'-res*], Montezuma. (E 1892; I 1900; P 820) For the river which flows through the city. Originally the town was about 1½ miles down river and known as Big Bend (for a river curve). With the coming of the Rio Grande Southern Railroad, the present townsite was established and named. The full Spanish name of the river, given by Father Escalente in 1776, was Rio de Nuestra Senora de las Dolores (River of Our Lady of Sorrows).

Dotsero, Eagle. (E 1880) There is no doubt George Yost filed a Dotsero town site plat in 1885; there is doubt about the name's origin. It is claimed on good authority this place was the starting point of the 1885 survey, and showed on the plats as .0 (dot zero), which later translated into Dotsero. Legend has it the name is that of an Indian chief's daughter. Another version: a Ute word for "something new," referring to a nearby, extinct volcano. It is also said there is no letter "d" in the Ute language.

Dove Creek, Dolores. (E 1918; I 1939; P 619) County seat. For a nearby stream, which, in turn, was named by an early freighter for the flocks of wild doves in the vicinity.

Dowd, Eagle. (E 1907 ?) For Jim Dowd, who opened a sawmill four miles up Mill Creek, a tributary of Gore Creek at Vail. The Denver & Rio Grande Railroad put in a spur at the junction of Gore Creek and the Eagle River to load lumber Dowd hauled to that point. There was no community established at the 3-car siding, which was named for Dowd.

Doyleville, Gunnison. (E 1879) For Henry Doyle, who established a stage line in a cattle and sheep raising town formerly known as Crooksville, and renamed in 1885. Also known as Doylestown and Doyle.

Drake, Larimer. (E 1902 ?) For State Sen. William A. Drake, who represented the district from 1903-1907, and who was instrumental in establishing a post office (1905). Locally referred to as The Forks as the location is at the junction of the North Fork of the Big Thompson River with the main stream. (Not to be confused with another Larimer County community known as The Forks.)

Dumont [*Doo'-mahnt*], Clear Creek. (E 1860) For John M. Dumont, mine owner, who undertook the revival of the town and its neighboring mines. It was first named Mill City, at the delta of Mill Creek, and was a settlement of ore-crushing mills. When the town was rejuvenated and postal facilities restored, there was another camp in Colorado with the name of Mill City.

Dunton, Dolores. (E 1892) For Horatio Dunton, owner of several thermal hot springs in the vicinity of the community. The founding date actually is the year a post office was established. When it was discontinued is unknown, but possibly before 1900.

Dupont [*Doo'-pahnt*], Adams. (P.O. E 1926) For the DuPont de Nemours family and the company of the same name (familiarly known as the Dupont Co.). The firm had several buildings here where explosives were stored. The name is French and is said to be derived from a reference to "of the bridge." (See: Louviers, Colo.)

Durango [*Doo-rang'-oh*], La Plata. (E 1880; I 1881; P 10,333) County seat. Named by former Territorial Gov. A.C. Hunt who had recently returned from a visit to Durango, Mexico. The origin of the word is not Spanish, but Basque, and was the name of a town in the Basque Province of northern Spain. In ancient Basque the word is Urango, signifying "water town." The addition of the "D" is said to show the Spanish influence.

Eads [*Eeds*], Kiowa. (E 1887; I 1916; P 795) County seat. For James B. Eads, a noted engineer who built the Eads Bridge across the Mississippi River at St. Louis. Eads was founded when the Missouri Pacific Railroad was extended through this area—but about three miles south of the present site—and called Dayton. When the railroad failed to reach Dayton the town—buildings and all—moved to the present location and renamed Eads.

Eagle, Eagle. (E 1887; I 1905; P 790) County seat. First called Castle for nearby Castle Mountain. Later the Denver & Rio Grande Western Railroad changed it to Rio Aquilla (Spanish for Eagle River). Next it became known as McDonald, for the man who owned the townsite. The citizens did not like the name and changed it to Eagle. Exact reasons for the name are unknown; one version is it refers to the Eagle River which was so named because it has as many tributaries as there are feathers in an eagle's tail.

East Portal, Gilpin. (E 1925) Founded during construction of the 6.4 mile Moffat Tunnel through a shoulder of James Peak. It takes its name for its location at the eastern entrance of the tunnel.

Eastlake, Adams. (E 1911) For East Lake, about half a mile distant. The area has always been rolling farmland and sparsely settled. The name could be a family name or possibly a designation—as "east of Broomfield."

Eaton [*Ee'-tun*], Weld. (E 1888; I 1892; P 1,389) For Benjamin H. Eaton, fourth Governor of Colorado (1885-1887), a prominent builder of irrigation projects and founder of the town. First called Eatonton to avoid conflict with Easton in El Paso County.

Echo Lake, Clear Creek. (E 1921) Probably for the reflections usually seen in the still waters of this high lake. This is not a community, but part of Denver's Mountain Parks System. From Echo Lake (10,605 ft.) a road goes to Summit Lake and then to the crest of Mount Evans (14,264 ft.), 13th highest peak in Colorado. The highway is the highest auto road in the U.S.

Eckley [*Ek'-lee*], Yuma. (E 1889; I 1920; P 193) An adaptation of the name of Adam Eckles, at one time cattle foreman for a well-known northeastern Colorado cattleman, J.W. Bowles.

Edgewater, Jefferson. (E 1890; I 1904; P 4, 866) For its location on the shore of Sloan's Lake, once the largest lake in area (270 acres) on Colorado's eastern slope.

Edwards, Eagle. (E 1882) In honor of Melvin Edwards after he became Colorado Secretary of State in 1883. First known as Berry's Ranch, for Harrison Berry, owner of the townsite land. (Two sources agree on the preceding version. A third is that when a post office was established in 1887, it was called Edwards in honor of a post office inspector of that time, and that the railroad changed the name of the station from Berry's Ranch to Edwards in 1912.)

Egnar [*Egg'-ner*], San Miguel. (P.O. E. 1917) Reverse spelling of "range," and adopted after the range land was thrown open to homesteading and a post office was established. One account has it that the name Range was desired, but was already in use by another town.

El Moro [*El Moh'-roh*], Las Animas. (E 1876) Named for a spur of Denver & Rio Grande Railroad. The name is Spanish, meaning "the Moor"—a native of Morocco.

El Rancho, Jefferson. (E 1953) Established as a restaurant with the same name (Spanish for "The Ranch") by Ray Zipprich. A post office, a branch of Golden's, was opened in 1956.

Elbert [*El'-bert*], Elbert. (E 1882) For former Territorial Gov. Samuel H. Elbert (1873-74), who later served as Chief Justice of the Colorado Supreme Court. The town's name was taken from the county name. A post office at nearby Gomers Mills, opened in 1870, was moved and became the Elbert post office.

Eldora [*El-doh'-ruh*], Boulder. (E 1896) Established as a gold mining camp and called Eldorado (Spanish: "the golden"). When application was made for a post office there was a prior claim, and the present version was used. (See: Eldorado Springs.)

Eldorado Springs [*El-doh-rod'-oh*], Boulder. (E 1904) Thermal springs here were probably named for their location in the midst of a highly mineralized district. A legend of Spanish explorers was that an Indian ruler's custom was to daily gild his body with gold dust, washing it off in a lake near his dwelling. This mythical potentate, "El Dorado," in time came to be used for regions rich in gold. (See: Eldora.)

Elizabeth, Elbert. (E 1880; I 1890; P 493) Named by Gov. John Evans for his sister-in-law, Elizabeth Gray Kimbark Hubbard. The governor was seeking names for new towns along the line of the Denver & New Orleans Railroad, of which he was promoter and principal owner. In 1885 this line was reorganized as the Denver, Texas & Gulf Railroad.

Elk Springs, Moffat. (E 1884) Named in 1884 by A.G. Wallihan for the springs which were a watering place for large herds of elk. Wallihan was an early Colorado photographer and emphasized nature in his work.

Ellicott, El Paso. (E 1892 ?) For the first postmaster, George Ellicott, originally from England and more recently from Kansas.

Empire, Clear Creek. (E 1860; I 1882; P 249) For the nickname of New York state, home of the four men who founded the town. First called Valley City and later Empire City.

Englewood, Arapahoe. (E 1875; I 1903; P 33,695) Originally a pleasure resort owned by A.C. Fisk, and known as Fisk's Gardens. Later known as Orchard Place for a large apple orchard. When the town was incorporated residents adopted the name of Englewood, which seems to have been taken for an Illinois town near Chicago. The word is from the old English "wood ingle," a wooded nook or corner.

Erie, Weld and Boulder. (E 1871; I 1885; P 1,090) Founded as a coal mining camp, it is supposed to have taken its name from Erie, Pa.

Estes Park [*Es'-tiz*], Larimer. (E 1905; I 1917; P 1,616) Earlier known as Estes Park Village, it was named for the first permanent settler, Joel Estes, who came to Estes Park in 1859 and built a cabin on Fish Creek.

Evans, Weld. (E 1869; I 1885; P 2,570) Laid out by the Denver Pacific Railroad and named for the second Colorado Territorial Governor, John Evans (1862-65). Evans was a leader in the financing and construction of the railroad. Earlier he was a founder of Northwestern University at Evanston, Ill. (named for him). In 1864, in Denver, he was a founder of the University of Denver.

Evergreen, Jefferson. (E 1866 ?) First called The Post, after Amos F. Post, son-in-law of Thomas Bergen, first settler of nearby Bergen Park in 1859. In 1875 D.P. Wilmot arrived in the area and acquired much land which is now Evergreen. He was pleased and impressed with the huge evergreen trees that he started calling the section, including The Post, Evergreen. The name has remained.

Fairplay, Park. (E 1859; I 1872; P 419) County seat. Founded by gold seekers who were angered to find the best placers at nearby Tarryall diggings taken. They found other rich deposits and established their own camp, called Fair Play as a jeer at their rivals' camp which they nicknamed "Graball." Fairplay—officially one word—was once known as South Park City.

Falcon. El Paso. (E 1887). Name probably suggested by the numerous brown and white prairie falcons (a species of hawk) native to the area. The falcon (bird) has been the mascot for the cadets of the United States Air Force Academy, north of Colorado Springs, since 1955.

Farisita [*Faris'-eet-uh*], Huerfano. (E ca. 1855) Referred to as Huerfano Canyon as early as 1850 by settlers and travelers who used the Taos Trail over Sangre de Cristo Pass. Later known as Talpa but changed because of the same name in New Mexico. Postmaster Asperidon S. Faris suggested the nickname of his little daughter, Jeanette. The Spanish people called her "Farisita" (little Faris girl). The name was adopted, according to the now adult Farisita (who still lives in the area), in 1921. The post office says the name change was 1923.

Federal Heights, Adams. (E 1940; I 1940; P 1,502) For its location on Federal Boulevard, north of Denver. Federal Boulevard is a major north-south thoroughfare in the western portion of Denver.

Firestone, Cheyenne. (E 1907; I 1908; P 570) Founded by the Denslow Coal & Land Co. and named for Jacob Firestone, owner of the townsite land. The coal-mining towns of Firestone, Dacono, and Frederick are called the "tri-cities," because they lie on a straight line along the Union Pacific Railroad and are so close together their boundaries overlap, according to *Colorado Magazine*.

Firstview, Cheyenne. (E 1870) Founded when the Kansas Pacific Railroad entered Colorado. It is a point where travelers from the east get their first glimpse of Pikes Peak and the Front Range of the Rockies. The Union Pacific Railroad later absorbed the K-P.

Flagler [*Flag'-ler*], Kit Carson. (E 1887; I 1916; P 615) For Henry M. Flagler, millionaire railroad man, who extended the Rock Island Railroad through this area. Originally the name was Malowe, for M.A. Lowe, attorney for the Rock Island. Prior to the platting of the site, there had been a combined store and post office managed by a man named Robinson, who called his post office "Bowser," in memory of a favorite dog that had died.

Fleming, Logan. (E 1889; I 1917; P 349) Originally a siding on the Chicago, Burlington & Quincy Railroad and known as Twenty-nine Mile Siding. The present site, half a mile from the original siding, was laid out in 1889 by H.B. Fleming, a representative of the Lincoln Land Co., and was named for him.

Florence, Fremont. (E 1872; I 1887; P 2,846) Founded in 1860 the town was known as Frazerville, for "Uncle Joe" Frazer who developed coal mines on nearby Coal Creek. Later the name was changed to Florence, to honor the daughter of James A. McCandless. He was the first to refine oil here (1862) and in 1872 gave the community its first real impetus to growth by donating a townsite and have the first town plat made. The second oldest oil field in the United States is in the Florence area.

Florissant [*Floh'-ri-sunt*], Teller. (E 1870) Named by Judge James Costello, the first settler, for his home town, Florissant, Mo. The region, once the bed of an ancient lake, is noted for its fossil remains.

Fort Collins, Larimer. (E 1872; I 1883; P 43,337) County seat. Although organized as a town in 1872, it started as an Army camp in 1864 with two companies of the 11th Ohio Volunteer Cavalry from Fort Laramie, Wyo. The site was called Camp Collins in honor of Col. W.O. Collins, commander at Fort Laramie. Later the post was known as Fort Collins. The settlement which had grown up around the fort kept the name after the military post was abandoned.

Fort Garland, Costilla. (E 1858) For John Garland, commander of the military district at the time the post was founded in 1858. Kit Carson was a commander here from 1866-67. The post was abandoned in 1883, but the name was retained by the settlement that had grown around it.

Fort Lewis, La Plata. (E 1877) First established at the present site of Pagosa Springs and named for a Lieutenant Colonel Lewis—a descendant of Meriwether Lewis, of the Lewis & Clark Expedition of 1804-06. In 1880 the post was moved about 12 miles southwest of present Durango, but abandoned a few years later.

Fort Lupton, Weld. (E 1882; I 1890; P 2,489) Founded by Lancaster P. Lupton, a lieutenant in the expedition of Col. Henry Dodge to the Rocky Mountains in 1835. Lupton took a leave from the Army and established a trading post in 1836 or 37, first calling it Fort Lancaster. The post was abandoned in the early 1840s but later the adobe building was used as a stage station on the mail and express route from Missouri to Denver.

Fort Lyon, Bent. (E 1860 ?) In 1853 Col. William Bent, after abandoning his great trading post on the Arkansas River, moved downstream about 40 miles and established a second post called Bent's New Fort. It was leased to the Army and renamed Fort Fauntleroy for a colonel of the First Dragoons. In 1859 the government purchased the site and renamed in Fort Wise, for Henry Wise, Governor of Virginia. Later it was again renamed in honor of Gen. Nathaniel Lyon, first Union soldier killed in the Civil War. In 1866 the river cut away the bank and a new Fort Lyon was built about 20 miles upriver. Kit Carson died on the reservation May 23, 1868.

Fort Morgan, Morgan. (E 1884; I 1887; P 7, 594) County seat. In honor of Col. Christopher A. Morgan of the United States Volunteers. The former military post was first known as Camp Tyler, but in 1865 renamed Fort Wardwell. The following year substantial buildings were erected and the name changed again, to its present one.

Fosston [*Fos'-tun*], Weld. (E 1909) Platted by H.W. Foss, a settler who also named the community using his own name. Foss originally came from England.

Fountain, El Paso. (E 1870; I 1903; P 3,515) For Fountain Creek, which flows through the town. Early French explorers called it La Fontaine Qui Bouille ("the spring that boils") because of its bubbling springs at its head. In 1888 the town was almost totally destroyed by the explosion of a carload of giant powder on the Denver & Rio Grande Railroad track here. The complete settlement of claims against the railroad enabled the town to rebuild itself.

Fowler, Otero. (E 1887; I 1900; P 1,241) Named for Professor O.S. Fowler, a phrenologist, when the town was platted in 1887. Earlier known as South Side, then Oxford Siding, and Sibley.

Foxton, Jefferson. (E 1876) First named Park Siding by Dr. Alvin Morey, the first settler, because of its park-like appearance. In 1909 the name was changed by J.O. Roach, a merchant, to Foxton. Supposedly the name was derived from Foxhall, a village in England.

Franktown, Douglas. (E 1861 ?) First known as California Ranch and later called Frankstown, honoring James Frank Gardner who owned the site on Cherry Creek. Postal authorities later deleted the "s." When Douglas County was created in 1861, Franktown was made the county seat, but lost the honor to Castle Rock in 1875. The original site is about five miles distant from the present town. It was once a camp site of John C. Fremont (1848), and once was also called Russellville, for Green Russell, early discoverer of gold in the area.

Fraser [*Fray'-zher*], Grand. (E 1871; I 1953; P 221) Formerly known as Easton, for George Easton, who laid out the townsite. Its present name is derived from that of the Fraser River which flows through the town. The spelling was originally Frazier—for Reuben Frazier, early settler—but postal authorities adopted the simpler spelling when the post office was established. When cold temperatures were regularly issued from Fraser, it had the reputation as "the icebox of the nation" because of the extremely low mercury readings.

Frederick [*Fred'-rick*], Weld. (E 1907; I 1908; P 696) Named for Frederick A. Clark, owner of the townsite land. Founded by three women, Mary M. Clark, Maud Clark Reynolds, and Mary Clark Steele. With Firestone and Dacono, it is one of the "tri-cities."

Frisco, Summit. (E 1879; I 1880; P 471) For San Francisco, California. The first settler was H.A. Recen, who arrived in 1873. Where Recen arrived from is not recorded—but, presumably, San Francisco.

Fruita [*Froo'-tuh*], Mesa. (E 1884; I 1894; P 1,822) The site selected by William E. Pabor, in 1883, who did much to advertise the fruit section of the western part of the state.

Galatea [*Guh-luh-tee'-uh*], Kiowa. (E 1887) Thought to have been named for the heroine of Cervantes's novel, *Saevedra,* who was also the heroine of a Greek legend.

Galeton, Weld. (E 1909) When the Union Pacific Railroad constructed a branch here, it chose Gale as the name for the station. Confusion with the nearby town of Gill brought the change to Galeton. An earlier name was Zita. The name probably honors a railroad official.

Garcia [*Gar-see'-uh*], Costilla. (E 1849) First called Manzanares, many early settlers were interrelated families by the name of Garcia. They named their post office Los Garcias of "The Garcias." The "Los" and final "s" have been dropped, leaving the present name. The town was once part of Costilla, N.M., which was settled somewhat earlier by people from the vicinity of Taos.

Garden City, Weld. (E 1935; I 1936; P 142) Name probably suggested by the nickname of nearby Greeley, "Garden City of the West." Earlier attempts to incorporate failed as the laws of Greeley prohibited sale of intoxicants, and it was asserted the purpose of this incorporation of the new town was to defeat the prohibition by providing a nearby supply.

Gardner, Huerfano. (E 1871 ?) In 1872 Herbert Gardner, son of Henry J. Gardner, former governor of Massachusetts, started ranching in the Huerfano Valley. The town was named for the Gardner family. Postal records indicate a post office in 1871 as Huerfano Canyon, changed the same year to Gardner.

Garfield, Chaffee. (E 1880) Originally founded as Junction City, the name was later changed by the postal department to avoid mail confusion with another Junction City. The present name honors President James A. Garfield.

Garo Park [*Gah'roe*], Park. (E 1863) Founded by Adolph Guiraud, one of the first sheepmen in the state. Guiraud, born in France, came to Colorado in the early 1860s. The town was named for him; a phonetic spelling of the French name resulting in Garo.

Gateway, Mesa. (E 1890) Selected because of its location at the "gateway" of the old Ute Trail into the mountainous country to the southwest and northeast.

Gem Village, La Plata. (E 1942) Founded by Frank Morse, who was in the gem and mineral business in Bayfield, Colo. He established a colony for artists and artisans and it became a rock hunter's haven for collectors and workers in semi-precious stones.

Genoa [*Gen'-oh-uh*], Lincoln. (E 1888; I 1905; P 161) Origin not certain, but believed to be named for Genoa, Italy. Earlier called Creech, for one of the contractors for the Rock Island Lines Railroad, and later Cable, for R.R. Cable, president of the Rock Island.

Georgetown, Clear Creek. (E 1864; I 1885; P 542) County seat. After gold was discovered by the Griffith brothers, David and George, in 1859, two camps developed near each other. One was Georgetown, for George Griffith, and the other Elizabethtown, for a Griffith sister. In a public meeting the two camps were united under the present name.

Gilcrest [*Gil'-crest*], Weld. (E 1908; I 1912; P 382) Originally a side-track and sugar beet dump called Nantes. W. K. Gilcrest bought large amounts of land here and organized a bank. He named the town Gil-crest, in honor of his father. The elder Gilcrest owned lumber yards in Des Moines, Iowa, and furnished financial backing for the Colorado bank.

Gill, Weld. (E 1909) For William H. Gill, president of the Gill-Deckers Improvement Co. The company sold 73 acres of land to the Union Pacific Railroad which built a depot and named the prospective town.

Gilman. Eagle. (E 1886) In honor of H.M. Gilman, a prominent early-day mining man. First founded as Clinton, and later named Battle Mountain, and Rock Creek.

Glade Park, Mesa. (E 1910) Because the top of adjacent Pinon Mesa opens into a large, flat park, which is heavily wooded.

Gladstone, San Juan. (E 1878 ?) For the noted British Prime Minister. Once the rail head of a spur-line called the Silverton-Northern, running from Silverton in 1899. The name may reflect British financial involvement in the area.

Glen Haven, Larimer. (E 1903) Named by Presbyterian School Missionary William H. Schureman for the peaceful surroundings. The Presbyterian Assembly Assn. purchased the land, settled by Orren S. Knapp in 1897, as a summer home resort. The community is at the foot of Devil's Gulch, a term the missionary felt was blasphemous.

Glendale, Arapahoe. (E 1952; I 1952; P 765) No known specifics except both "glen" and "dale" describe rolling, pleasant country. The name for this Denver enclave was probably chosen for its euphonic sound. The community was established to prevent annexation to Denver.

Glendevey [*Glen-day'-vee*], Larimer. (E 1902) Former Mississippi River skipper, Thomas (Cap) Davy, bought a ranch in a glen. He called the post office , established on the property, Glen Davy. In later years the name was changed to Glendevey. The post office site was moved about four times before it eventually closed. Since 1974 the summer resort's mail address is now Glendevey Colorado Route, Jelm, Wyoming, 82063.

Glenwood Springs, Garfield. (E 1882; 1885 P. 4,106) County seat. First called Glenwood Hot Springs (later shortened) for Glenwood, Iowa, and for the mineral springs in the vicinity. Also once called Defiance.

Golden, Jefferson. (E 1859; I 1886; P 9,817) County seat. For Thomas L. Golden, who, with James Saunders and George W. Jackson, established a temporary camp near the mouth of Clear Creek Canyon in 1858. Though they took preliminary steps toward laying out a townsite, the city was actually established by the Boston Co., headed by George West. From 1862 to 1867 it was the capital of Colorado Territory.

Goodrich, Morgan. (E 1882) For Gus T. Goodrich, a Morgan County pioneer and member of the first Board of County Commissioners, when the Union Pacific Railroad built a spur here in 1882.

Gould [*Gool'-d*], Jackson. (E 1936) For Edward B. Gould, who settled a homestead in 1898. The community of Gould started with the sale of a large timber tract in North Park and a store was opened, as was a post office. Earlier, an informal community in the area was known as Penfold. Gould as a town is now non-existent, and the site is in private hands.

Granada [*Gron-aid'-uh*], Prowers. (E 1873; I 1887; P 551) Created by the Atchison, Topeka & Santa Fe Railway when the line was extended to this point. After the rail head pushed on to La Junta, the town was moved to its present site in 1876. Originally it had been at the mouth of Granada Creek, for which it was named, probably for the city and former kingdom of Spain. Washington Irving popularized it in his *Conquest of Granada,* (1829).

Granby [*Gran'-bee*], Grand. (E 1904; I 1905; P 554) Named for Granby Hillyer, a Denver attorney. It is presumed Hillyer was associated with the founding of the community in some major capacity. (The origin is disputed by some—but no substitute suggestion has been made.)

Grand Junction, Mesa. (E 1881; I 1882, P 20,170) County seat. Named for its location at the junction of the Gunnison and Grand (later Colorado) Rivers. Earlier known as Ute after the Grand Valley, under a treaty with the Ute Indians, was declared public land in 1881.

Grand Lake, Grand. (E 1879; I 1944; P 189) For Grand Lake, largest natural body of water in Colorado, after it was founded as a mining settlement by the Grand Lake Town & Improvement Co., made up of Kentuckians. Now a popular summer resort.

Grand Valley, Garfield. (E 1886; I 1908; P 270) Named for the Valley of the Grand (now Colorado) River. First known as Parachute, for Parachute Creek on which it is located. That name is derived from the East, West, and Middle Forks of the creek which, from on high, resemble the shrouds of a parachute. In Spring, 1976, a proposal to return to the name of Parachute was defeated at the polls. In anticipation of the change, however, the name appeared for one year on the state map and in the index. (The first human parachute descent was made from a balloon, in France, in 1797.)

Granite, Chaffee. (E 1860 ?) Probably for the barren, rocky granite outcroppings in the vicinity. The old gold-mining camp was once the seat of Lake County, and the temporary seat of Chaffee County after it was formed.

Grant, Park. (E 1870) Probably for President Ulysses S. Grant. Also once known as Grantville.

Great Divide, Moffat. (E 1916) Believed to have been named for the *Great Divide,* a weekly publication once issued by *The Denver Post,* from 1914-18. The community had a *Great Divide Sentinel* in 1917-18.

Greeley, Weld. (E 1870; I 1885; P 38,902) County seat. For Horace Greeley of the *New York Tribune,* who was impressed with the agricultural possibilities of the country when he visited the West in 1859. When his agricultural editor, Nathan C. Meeker, made a trip west he conceived a plan to found a colony and Greeley began a publicity campaign in his paper. The Union Colony was adopted and bought a townsite, which was named in Greeley's honor.

Green Mountain Falls, El Paso-Teller. (E 1889; I 1890; P 359) For a series of cascades cutting the side of nearby Green Mountain.

Greenwood Village, Arapahoe. (E 1950; I 1950; P 2,578) Named for its once wooded terrain. The residents became apprehensive about encroachment of undesirable housing and business developments. They incorporated so that, through zoning regulations, the residential and farming community aspects would be preserved.

Greystone, Moffat. (E 1882 ?) In the Brown's Hole area, a former hiding place for cattle rustlers and "bad men." In 1921, Henry Kenealy, the first postmaster, named the place Greystone for the grey rocks in the vicinity.

Grover, Weld. (E 1888; I 1916; P 121) Named by Mrs. Neal Donovan, pioneer settler, who gave it her maiden name. The first post office was called Catoga, about a mile north of the present town.

Guffy, Park. (E 1890 ?) An early gold-mining camp first called Idaville, then Freshwater, and finally Guffy. It takes its name from J.K. Guffey, a pioneer settler, but along the way the "e" was dropped from the official spelling.

Gulnare [*Gull-nair'*], Las Animas. (E 1884) Once known as Abeyton, but the post office was taken from the postmaster for some irregularity. A new name was to be decided, and names were submitted to postal authorities in Washington. On the envelope in which these were mailed was the picture of a blooded Holstein cow with her name, "Princess of Gulnare." The post office discarded the submitted names and selected Gulnare.

Gunnison, Gunnison. (E 1880; I 1880; P 4,613) County seat. First known as Richardson's Colony. In 1879, Governor Evans and others organized the Gunnison Town Co. A survey was made and plat filed in 1880. The place, on the Gunnison River, was named for Capt. J.W. Gunnison, who, in 1853, led a surveying party through the area in search of a railroad route to the west. Gunnison and most of his company were killed by Ute Indians in Utah in the fall of the same year.

Gypsum [*Jip'-sum*], Eagle. (E 1887; I 1911; P 420) For the large deposits of gypsum found in the region.

Hahns Peak [*Honn'-s*], Routt. (E 1864) Now a group of decaying buildings, this was once a booming gold town and the county seat. Joseph Henne—or Henn—a German, led a party of prospectors. Two camps arose, one Bug Town because of the wealthy people or "big bugs," the other Poverty Bar. The latter became Hahns Peak. Hahn was a corruption of the name Henne. Henne—Hahn—lost his life in a blizzard in 1867.

Hale, Yuma. (E 1887) The first store—and post office—was operated by a Richard Taylor, a Civil War veteran. It is believed he named it for one of his heroes, Nathan Hale, early American patriot.

Hamilton, Moffat. (E 1885) For Tom and Riley Hamilton, early settlers. No other details seem recorded concerning these pioneers.

Hartman, Prowers. (E 1906; I 1910; P 129) Because of a clerical error in the Chicago offices of the Santa Fe Railway, the town was named for George Hartman, a former company superintendent. The intention had been to name it for C.H. Bristol, an assistant general manager of the road, who owned land near Hartman. At the same time, the town of Bristol, near which Hartman owned property, was named for Bristol. The mistake was never corrected. (See: Bristol, Colo.)

Hartsel [*Hart'-sul*] , Park. (E 1866) For Samuel Hartsel, pioneer cattleman, who came to the region from Pennsylvania about 1860. Hartsel was unable to find gold and began buying travel-worn oxen from wagon trains coming in from the East. He fattened, rested, and resold the animals to travelers returning East. Later he acquired pure-bred shorthorns and founded the stock-raising industry in South Park.

Hasty, Bent. (E 1907) First homesteaded in 1886, it was settled in 1907 by W.A. Hasty and George Hill. A townsite was laid out and the Santa Fe Railway named the settlement for Hasty. In 1939 the town started to grow as it was near the site of the big Caddoa Dam project.

Haswell [*Has'-well*], Kiowa. (E 1905; I 1920; P 135) Jay Gould's daughter gave to a number of consecutive stations on Gould's Missouri Pacific Railroad, names with the initial letters in alphabetical order as one approached Pueblo from the east. The origin of some—such as Haswell—is now unknown. The stations so named were: Arden, Brandon, Chivington, Diston, Eada, Fergus, Galaton, Haswell, Inman, Jolliett, Kilburn, Lolita, Meredity, Nepesta, Olney, and Putney. Several names no longer are in use. Another version is that the residents were so happy to strike water the name comes from "has a well."

Hawley, Otero. (E 1908) Originally a beet dump for the American Beet Sugar Co. of Rocky Ford. It was named about 1908 for Floyd Hawley, who for years was cashier of the sugar firm.

Haxtun, Phillips. (E 1888; I 1909; P 899) Established when the Burlington Railroad built a line here in 1888. The name honors one of the railroad contractors. By mistake, the name was spelled Haxtum, and some early maps use Haxton. The correct orthography is Haxtun.

Hayden [*Hay'-dun*], Routt. (E 1894; I 1906; P 763) The first houses here were built in 1875 by a Maj. J. B. Thompson, Col. P. M. Smart and two sons. They named the settlement in honor of Ferdinand V. Hayden, then head of the U.S. Geological & Geographic Survey. Hayden did a survey of Colorado starting in the late 1860s.

Heartstrong, Yuma. (E 1920) Founded by Cleve Mason, who earlier (1908) founded and owned Happyville, two miles east. After selling Happyville to a cooperative, he built another store, garage, and filling station. Friction between Mason and the co-op made Mason decide to move to a new location. The name Heartstrong is unexplained. It's possible it means "strong of heart" reflecting on his tenacity to stay in business. The dust bowl days of the 1930's depleted the population, and fire destroyed the last building in 1940.

Heeney, Summit. (E 1938) For Paul Heeney, owner of much land bordering Green Mountain dam when it was built in 1938.

Henderson, Adams. (E 1859) For Capt. (sometimes called Colonel) Jack Henderson, an early freighter. He reached Auraria (Denver) with a wagon train of supplies in 1858. On a parcel of land in the Platte River he set up the first feed yard and public corral in the region. The island became known as Henderson's Island, and the community which grew up along the river bank also took Henderson's name.

Hereford [*Her'-ferd*], Weld. (E 1902) For the famous breed of white-faced cattle popular in the region since early days. A Hereford station was established by the Burlington Railroad in 1886, just north of the Colorado line. In 1888 a post office of the same name was created in Weld County. In 1902, Frank Benton named his ranch and small settlement in Colorado "New Hereford," but the "new" was later dropped. A town plat was filed in 1909.

Hermosa, La Plata. (E 1874 ?) A station on the Denver & Rio Grande Western Railroad line to Silverton. The founders are said to have selected the name—a Spanish word meaning "pretty"—as descriptive of its location. While a post office was established in 1874, no mail was delivered until the following year when the first mail was brought over the range from Howardsville by snowshoers.

Hesperus [*Hes'-puh-ruhs*], La Plata. (E 1882) Settled in 1882 with the opening of the Hesperus Coal Mine by John A. Porter, it was named by the Rio Grande Southern Railroad for Mount Hesperus, 12 miles northwest of town. The mountain probably was named using the Latin word for Venus, the Evening Star.

Hiawatha, Moffat. (E 1926 ?) For the nearby Hiawatha oil field camp. The name is probably from Longfellow's poem rather than the original character of mythology. The camp was closed in 1968.

Hideaway Park, Grand. (E 1905 ?) For its hidden location, with pine trees effectively screening it from the highway. Earlier thought to be known first as Woodstock. The name Vasquez was used for several years, and it was also called Little Chicago. A Max Kortz, who owned a dance hall in the village, is believed to have applied the present name. Records are scarce and even post office records fail to show an early date for postal service.

Hillrose, Morgan. (E 1900; I 1919; P121) Settled by the Lincoln Land Co., the Burlington Railroad's townsite corporation. Mrs. Kate Emerson of Denver, who had deeded land for the townsite, was permitted by the railroad to select the town's name. She reversed her sister's name, Rose Hill, to make Hillrose.

Hillside, Fremont. (E 1880 ?) Mrs. Seth Brown, postmistress in 1884, called the settlement after the family's ranch, Hillside. Prior to this the post office was called Texas Creek.

Hoehne [*Hoe-knee*], Las Animas. (E 1886) For William Hoehne, a German pioneer settler who came to the region in the 1860s. Known as "Dutch Bill," Hoehne built the first mill and irrigation ditch, the beginning of extensive irrigation in the area. The Hoehne post office was moved from Pulaski, where it had opened in 1874.

Holly, Prowers. (E 1896; I 1903; P 993) For Hiram S. Holly, pioneer rancher, who established the SS Ranch, which originally extended from Granada to the Kansas border. The lowest point in Colorado (3,350 ft.) is near Holly. (3,397 ft.).

Holyoke [*Holy'-ohk*], Phillips. (E 1887; I 1888; P 1,640) County seat. For Holyoke, Mass., which in turn had been named for the Rev. Edward Holyoke, an early president of Harvard College. Phillips County was established in 1889 from the southern part of Logan County. It was then Holyoke became the county seat.

Homelake, Rio Grande. (E 1890) Created as the State Soldiers and Sailors Home on land donated by the town of Monte Vista, on what was called Stanger Lake (now Homelake). The first buildings were opened and dedicated to Civil War veterans in November, 1891. In 1965 the Colorado Legislature passed an act changing the name to Colorado State Veterans Center.

Hooper, Alamosa. (E 1891; I 1898; P 80) First called Garrison, attributed to the mercantile firm of Garrison & Howard. Confusion resulted between the names of Gunnison and Garrison. The latter was changed to Hooper, for Maj. S. Hooper, passenger agent for the Denver & Rio Grande Railroad.

Hot Sulphur Springs, Grand. (E 1860; I 1903; P 220) County seat. Named for the hot springs in the area. Townsite once owned by William N. Byers, founder of the Denver *Rocky Mountain News.* An earlier proposal to locate a town was abandoned; this was to have been named Saratoga West, after the noted watering place in New York.

Hotchkiss, Delta. (E 1881; I 1901; P 507) For Enos Hotchkiss, who was an early settler.

Howard, Fremont. (E 1880 ?) For John Howard, who settled on a creek in 1876 that came to bear his name. In 1880 the Denver & Rio Grande Western Railroad built its right-of-way and a station on the Arkansas River nearly opposite the mouth of Howard Creek, naming the station Howard.

Hoyt, Morgan. (E 1882 ?) This hamlet was the original homestead of Mrs. Sidney Davis Hoyt, who settled with her sons, Edwin G. and Dr. James A. The latter, in addition to being a doctor, was also a surveyor and did considerable railroad surveying. The town was named for him.

Hudson, Weld. (E 1887; I 1914; P 518) For the Hudson City Land & Improvement Co. of Denver, who purchased and developed the townsite.

Hugo [*Hyoo'-goh*], Lincoln. (E 1874; I 1909; P 759) County seat. Supposedly for a pioneer settler named Richard Hugo. Another source reports the town was named for French novelist Victor Hugo.

Hygiene [*High'-jeen*], Boulder. (E 1861) After an early sanitarium, Hygiene Home, established by a Dunkard preacher, Jacob S. Flory. A group from Pella, Iowa, settled near the present town and called the place Pella. A post office later was moved northeast and the settlement called North Pella. The Reverend Flory built between the two Pellas, and was the first postmaster of the town which absorbed the two Pellas and became Hygiene.

Idaho Springs, Clear Creek. (E 1860; I 1885; P 2,003) An outgrowth of the camp of George A. Jackson, who discovered gold in the area in 1859. The meaning of the name is controversial. One version is a derivation from an Indian word meaning "gem of the mountains;" another translates it as "rocks." It may have come from "Idahi," the Kiowa-Apache name for the Comanches. In addition to Jackson's Diggings, the town has been known as Sacramento City, Idaho City, and Idaho or Idahoe. The name Idaho was once proposed for Colorado Territory.

Idalia [*Eye-dayl'-yuh*], Yuma. (E 1887) For Mrs. Edaliah Helmick, wife of one of the original settlers. The change in spelling was for simplification. Originally the site was about a half mile west of the present location. It was first known as Friend, for a town in Nebraska, from which some of the region's settlers came.

Idledale, Jefferson.(E 1905 ?) Founded by John C. Starbuck, first as a guest ranch, and later a popular summer-home community. Although named for Starbuck it was also known as Joyland in the 1920's. After a Bear Creek Canyon flood in 1932, destroying lives and property, in an effort to help erase the bad memories, the name was changed to Idledale. This was probably taken from Idledale Heights, part of "old Starbuck," reflecting unhurried summer living in the mountains.

Ignacio [*Ig-nass'-ee-oh*], La Plata. (E 1910; I 1913; P 613) For Chief Ignacio of the Utes. It was headquarters of the Southern Ute Indian Reservation and site of an Indian school and hospital. The town land was purchased from the tribe in 1910.

Iliff [*Eye'-liff*], Logan. (E 1881, I 1926, P 193). For John W. Iliff, early Colorado cattle king, whose L. F. Ranch embraced the townsite. Iliff's widow gave a large part of his estate to the founding of the Iliff School of Theology. The Iliff campus is adjacent to that of the University of Denver.

Indian Hills, Jefferson. (E 1925) Established by a realty firm, Associated Industries, as a summer resort. The name was probably chosen for its picturesque quality. Earlier, the area was known as Eaton Park.

Ivywild, El Paso. (E 1888) This Colorado Springs suburb was owned and platted by William B. Jenkins, and named by his wife. The name has no known historic significance; probably a coined word indicating quiet surroundings.

Jamestown, Boulder. (E 1864; I 1883; P 185) While the post office, established in 1867, was called Jamestown, the camp seems to have originally been known as Jimtown—possibly for an early settler's nickname. The mining camp was early called Elysian Park, because of its beautiful mountain setting. Jimtown still is the name used in the locality.

Jansen, Las Animas. (E 1900 ?) Probably for Jansen's Quarry which apparently became a settlement and station on the Santa Fe Railway and Colorado & Southern Railroad. Once known as Chimayoses.

Jarosa [*Hah-roh'-suh*], Costilla. (E 1914) A Spanish word meaning "bramble covered." A plat of the community was filed in 1914. While the name is spelled, correctly, as here, the state map and index shows it "Jaroso."

Jefferson, Park. (E 1861) Named for nearby Jefferson Lake and Jefferson Creek which in turn honor President Thomas Jefferson. Originally two settlements, Palestine and Jefferson, they soon united under the latter name.

Joes [*Johs*], Yuma. (E 1912) Established by C.N. White and Joseph White. Among the settlers were three men named Joe; the place was first called Three Joes, later shortened to its present form.

Johnson Village, Chaffee. (E 1947) Started as a cafe and service station by John Johnson at the U.S. 285 junction near Buena Vista. Others started buying property in the vicinity and the settlement began to be called Johnson Village. About 350 persons live in the immediate area, mostly in mobile home parks. The village first appeared on the state highway map in 1976.

Johnstown, Weld. (E 1902; I 1907; P 1,191) Laid out by a Harvey J. Parish, who named it for his son, John.

Julesburg, Sedgwick. (E 1884; I 1886; P 1,578) County seat. The last of four towns of the name. Originally a stage station at the ranch and trading post of Jules Beni, from which the town gets its name. The other sites were in the vicinity. Present Julesburg was located when the Union Pacific Railroad built a branch line to Denver. It was incorporated as Denver Junction in November, 1885, and as Julesburg the following year.

Karval [*Kar'-vel*], Lincoln. (E 1910) Homesteaded in 1910 by G.K. Kravig, who, with other settlers, petitioned for a post office, which was established in 1911. Postal authorities selected the name Karval, derived from the family name Kravig. Kravig was the first postmaster.

Kassler, Jefferson. (E 1872 ?) The site of a Denver water-filter plant on the South Platte River, the name is for E.S. Kassler, president of the Denver Union Water Co. from 1915-18. Originally known as Platte Canon, it was renamed Watertown in 1916, for the water works. Although shown as Kassler on the state map, the Waterton name is still on entrance signs at the tiny community. (See: Waterton.)

Keenesburg, Weld. (E 1907; I 1919; P 427) First known as Keene, for an area rancher, as a telegraph office and side track for the Chigago, Burlington & Quincy Railroad. When a post office was established in 1907, the present name was suggested.

Keota [*Kee'-oh-tuh*], Weld. (E 1888; I 1919; P 6) For an Indian term (tribe not specified) meaning "gone to visit" or "the fire has gone out."

Originally homesteaded by Mary E. Beardsley, who sold the site to the Lincoln Land Co. in 1888.

Kersey [*Ker'-see*], Weld. (E 1887; I 1908; P 474) With the building of the Union Pacific Railroad through here in 1882, a section house and station were erected and called Orr, in honor of James H. Orr, first colonist to pay the $155 fee for Union Colony land. The name was often confused with Orr, Calif., and Carr, Colo., so was renamed in 1896 by Roadmaster John K. Painter, for his mother's maiden name. The first real settlement started about 1887, by H.P. Hill and D.E. Gray.

Kim, Las Animas. (E 1918; I 1974; P 300) For Kipling's famous boy hero, Kim. First established about 1893 but because the settlers knew little about dry-land farming, the project failed. In 1918 Olin D. Simpson started the present town and built a post office-store on a corner of his homestead.

Kiowa [*Kigh'-oh-wuh*], Elbert. (E 1869; I 1912; P 235) County seat. Named for the Kiowa Indian tribe. Once was known as Middle Kiowa.

Kirk, Yuma. (E 1883) The town was founded by A. Nekirk, and the town's name is an abbreviation of his. A post office was established four miles north of the present site in 1888, but two years later when another postmaster was named, the office was moved to his homestead, the present location.

Kit Carson, Cheyenne. (E 1869; I 1931; P 220) For the famous western scout and guide. The original town was three miles west of its present site, on the banks of Sand Creek, and the terminus of the Kansas Pacific Railroad. (See: Kit Carson County.)

Kittredge [*Kit'-ridge*], Jefferson. (E 1920) Established when the Kittredge Town Co. purchased the Luther Ranch of some 300 acres. Charles M. Kittredge applied for a post office in 1921, suggesting it be called Bear Creek. There was already an office by that name, and postal officials decided to name the settlement for the Kittredge family, which had lived in the vicinity since 1860.

Kline, La Plata. (E 1904) Name originated from a Mormon colony that settled the town and obtained a post office. The meaning of the name is unknown, but possibly the name of a founder or a church leader. Although Kline had a post office, a later, nearby town, Marvel, outgrew it. Marvel mail was received at Kline until the post office was moved to Marvel in 1953. (See: Marvel, Colo.)

Kornman, Prowers. (E 1908 ?) A station on the Atchison, Topeka & Santa Fe Railway, it was named for Charles Kornman, a local landowner.

Kremmling, Grand. (E 1881; I 1904; P 764) The town's beginning was a general merchandise store run by Kare Kremmling, located on the Dr. Harris ranch on the north bank of the Muddy River. In 1888 John and Aaron Kinsey had part of their ranch platted, and called the site Kinsey City. Kremmling moved his store across the river to the new site which soon became known as Kremmling.

Kutch [*Koo'-ch*], Elbert. (E 1904) For Ira Kutch, cattleman. The post office village was formerly three miles south of the present site. The first post office was established as Sanborn in 1878.

La Garita [*Lah-guh-ree'-tuh*], Saguache. (E 1874 ?) for La Garita Peak, west of the town. The word is Spanish, meaning "the lookout," or, loosely, "the signal." Reportedly Indians sent smoke signals from La Garita Peak to the Sangre de Cristo Range, across the San Luis Valley.

La Jara [*Lah-Hair'-uh*], Conejos. (E 1880; I 1910; P 768) The Spanish name, literally "cistus or rock rose," is locally confused with "brush," and refers to the undergrowth along the banks of the river. Before there were real settlements between the Conejos River and Rio Grande, a few Mexican families lived near this site and the place was called Llano Blanco ("White plain").

La Junta [*La Hun'-tuh*], Otero. (E 1875; I 1881; P 7,938) County seat. Founded as the temporary stopping place of the Santa Fe Railway. Its first name, Otero, was retained until 1878, when the Kansas Pacific branch was abandoned and the Santa Fe extended south. La Junta, Spanish for "the junction," refers to the joining of the railroad lines.

La Plata [*La Plat'-uh*], La Plata. (E 1873) The Spanish word for "silver." Originally founded as Parrott City in honor of Tubucio Parrott, San Francisco banking house owner.

La Salle, Weld. (E 1910; I 1910; P 1,227) The existence of the town is supposed to be due to a quarrel between the Union Pacific Railroad and the city of Greeley. This led to La Salle's becoming the northern Colorado headquarters for the railroad in 1909-10. The name is said by some to honor the French explorer of the Mississippi River, and by others that it was given for La Salle, Ill., by a settler who had originally come from there.

La Veta [*La Vee'-tah*], Huerfano. (E 1876; I 1886; P 589) The Spanish name means "the vein" and probably refers here to the many dykes radiating in all directions from West Spanish Peak. It was formerly known as Francisco Plaza or Francisco Ranch, as Col. John M. Francisco selected this site for his home while on a prospecting tour in 1834.

Lafayette [*Lah-fay-et'*], Boulder. (E 1888; I 1890; P 3,498) For Lafayette Miller, husband of Mary E. Miller, owner of the townsite land.

Laird, Yuma. (E 1887) For Congressman James Laird of Nebraska. The town was surveyed and laid out by the See Bar See Land & Cattle Co.

Lake City, Hinsdale. (E 1875; I 1884; P 91) County seat. Name taken for nearby Lake San Cristobal (Spanish for "Saint Christopher"), one of the largest natural lakes in Colorado. It is the only community in the county—which is the state's least populated. (See: Hinsdale County.)

Lake George, Park. (E 1886) Pioneer rancher, George Frost, dammed the South Platte River as it came out of Eleven Mile Canyon, to form a lake from which to cut ice for the Colorado Midland Railroad. First called Lidderdale Reservoir, it was commonly known as George's Lake. When a post office was established in 1891 it became Lake George. The ice business helped the community flourish, but died when the railroad was abandoned in 1918. Prior to the railroad the site was an overnight stage stop between Colorado Springs and Leadville.

Lakeside, Jefferson. (E 1907; I 1907; P 4) Not on the state highway map, this tiny community is the home of Lakeside Amusement Park. The site was named for its location around a small lake, now within the amusement park. The location is at W. 46th Ave. and Sheridan Blvd. (Map location about E-17.)

Lakewood, Jefferson. (E 1872; I 1969; P 92,787) Probably for the fact the now-sprawling suburban area was the site of many orchards and small lakes, and early was largely agricultural. It started its "official" incorporated life as the third largest city in the state.

Lamar [*La-mar'*], Prowers. (E 1886; I 1886; P 7,797) County seat. Named for the Secretary of the Interior, L.Q.C. Lamar, at the time of its establishment.

Laporte [*Lah-port'*], Larimer. (E 1859) First called Colona, it was the first settlement in this region. In 1858 John B. Provost and Antoine Janis with a group of French trappers came from the trading post at Fort Laramie seeking a site for a new post. The name was changed to its present form in 1862 when a post office was established. La Porte is French for "the gate," and was given because its site is the natural gateway to the area lying to the northwest. The two words have been combined into one in recent years.

Larkspur, Douglas. (E 1865) The pretty larkspur flowers that covered the surrounding hills, suggested the name. The flower, however, is poisonous to livestock.

Las Animas [*Lahs-an'-i-muhs*], Bent. (E 1869; I 1886; P 3,148) County seat. After the building of a new Fort Lyon, a flourishing settlement grew up on the opposite side of the Arkansas River. The site, surveyed in 1869, was named for the Las Animas River: Rio de las Animas Perdidas in Purgatorio, ("the river of lost souls in purgatory"). When the Kansas Pacific Railroad built its branch from Kit Carson to the Arkansas River, the town of West Las Animas was settled six miles west of the first site. The name was changed to its present form in 1886.

Last Chance, Washington. (E 1926) Established by Essa Harbert and Archie Chapman in the days of the Model T Ford (and other vintage cars). The name reflects the fact it was (and still is) several miles in either direction on U.S. 36 for gas, oil, water, etc.

Lawson, Clear Creek. (E 1876) Once a solitary inn known as Six Mile House, owned by Alexander Lawson. When valuable ores were discoverd here in 1876 many prospectors came and a town soon developed. The community was named for the original settler.

Lay, Moffat. (E 1880) After the Meeker Massacre (1879-80) soldiers were stationed at various points to guard the road from Rawlins, Wyo., to protect supply trains. One squad, camped on a small creek, in charge of a Lieutenant McCullough (or McCulloch) who named the place Camp Lay, honoring his sweetheart in Chicago. The camp was abandoned, but later, when a post office was established, it was also called Lay. A. G. Wallihan established the present town about a mile west of the original location.

Lazear, Delta. (E 1910) For J.B. Lazear, a pioneer settler, after the town was founded by B.M. Stone as the supply point for the area's fruit and livestock districts.

Leadville [*Led'-vil*], Lake. (E 1878; I 1878; P 4,314) County seat. First silver strikes in this area were made in 1876-77 and a rush began. The early camp was known by many names; Slabtown, Boughtown, Cloud City, Carbonate, Harrison, Agassiz. When the time came for legal adoption of a name, controversy raged. One faction favored Harrison, for Harrison of the Harrison Reduction Works. Horace Tabor, storekeeper, favored Leadville, and prevailed. The name was chosen for the large amount of argentiferous lead ores in the vicinity.

Lebanon [*Leb'-uh-nun*], Montezuma. (E 1908) Built in a dense setting of cedars, as was the Biblical Lebanon, the village was founded and named by the Railway Building & Loan Co. of Pueblo.

Lewis [*Loo'-is*], Montezuma. (E 1909 ?) For W. R. Lewis, who purchased the townsite at the time of the settlement's establishment.

Limon [*Lie'-mun*], Lincoln. (E 1888; I 1909; P 1,814) Established as a camp for the Rock Island Railroad, it was known as Limon's Camp, for the foreman. Later, Limon's Junction, for a meeting of the Rock Island and Union Pacific Railroads. The present name was taken upon incorporation.

Lindon, Washington. (E 1888 ?) First known as Harrisburg. When the post office was moved three miles southeast, the name was changed to Linden, in honor of L.J. Lindbeck of Illinois, an early resident. When the present spelling was adopted is unknown.

Littleton, Arapahoe and Douglas. (E 1872; I 1890; P 26,466) County seat. Founded by and named for Richard Sullivan Little, a civil engineer from New Hampshire, who came to Colorado in 1860 and started farming. With J.C. Lilley he built the Rough & Ready Flouring Mills in 1867.

Livermore, Larimer. (E 1863) For two of the earliest permanent settlers: Adolphus Livernash and Stephen Moore, who built a cabin near the townsite and became prospectors. Even though Moore's name was changed in spelling, it is still a good example of an acronym.

Lochbuie [*Lock-boo'-ee*], Weld. (E 1960; I 1974; P 800) Established first as Space City and incorporated in 1974 as Lochbuie. The name Space City was derived from a house trailer court called Spacious Living, which provides most of the town's residences. Lochbuie is named for an area on the Isle of Mull in Scotland, where ancestors of one of the town's organizers lived.

Log Lane Village, Morgan. (E 1955; I 1955; P 329) First conceived as a site for a liquor store outside of "dry" Fort Morgan, and then expanded for a community. Originally every building, according to ordinance, was built from or sided with logs—hence the name. The ordinance was dropped in the mid 1960's.

Loma [*Loh'-muh*], Mesa. (E 1900 ?) A Spanish name meaning "hill in a plain."

Lonetree, Archuleta. (E 1895 ?) Probably for a natural landmark—a single tree, perhaps on a mountain or in a meadow. Physical or natural landmarks accounted for many settlement names.

Longmont, Boulder. (E 1871; I 1885; P 23,209) For nearby Longs Peak, whose name honors explorer Maj. Stephen H. Long. An old town of Burlington, founded years before, was merged with the new settlement. The town was founded by the Chicago-Colorado Colony, and the name was selected by the Colony members in Chicago.

Louisville [*Loo'-is-vil*], Boulder. (E 1878; I 1890; P 2,409) C.C. Welch of Golden discovered coal here in 1877. The boring was in charge of Louis Nawatny, who also owned the surface of the land on which the original settlement was located. Nawatny had the town platted and his name was adopted by the town.

Louviers [*Loo'-vers*], Douglas. (E 1906) Founded as the site of a branch explosives factory of the Du Pont industries, and named for Louviers, Del., where the Du Ponts established a woolen-cloth factory. The Delaware town, in turn, was named for the French city that is the center of the woolen industry in France. (See: Dupont, Colo.)

Loveland [*Luv'-land*], Larimer. (E 1877; I 1881; P 16,220) For W.A.H. Loveland, president of the Colorado Central Railroad, and prominent in state affairs. The townsite was platted on the farm of David Barnes—later known as the "father of Loveland"—and who declined to have the town named for him. Loveland's name also graces 11,992 ft. Loveland Pass on the Continental Divide.

Lucerne [*Loo-sern'*], Weld. (E 1892 ?) When the Union Pacific Railroad built a side track and station, for alfalfa and potatoes, the settlement was called Lucerne, the name by which alfalfa was commonly known.

Lycan [*Ligh'-cun*], Baca. (E 1910) Mabel Lycan and her Civil War veteran father, Morgan B.F. Tresner, homesteaded here in 1910. Their plan was to establish a community modeled after Tresner, Ill., which had been settled by the Tresner family. The Colorado town was named by the settlers for Mrs. Lycan, who was the first school teacher, and was post mistress for 20 years.

Lyons [*Ligh'-uns*], Boulder. (E 1882; I 1891; P 958) For Mrs. Carrie Lyons, pioneer editor of the *Lyons News*. The weekly newspaper existed only in 1890-91. The town was platted by the Lyons Town Site & Quarry Co. Quarrying superior sandstone was an early major industry.

Mack, Mesa. (E 1904) Founded by employees of the Uintah Railway who named it for John M. Mack, first president of Barber Asphalt Co., and builder of the railroad. The line was abandoned in 1939.

Maher [*May'-her*], Montrose. (E 1882) For Caleb Maher, first stage driver in the vicinity. When a post office was established in 1884, Maher was named postmaster.

Malta [*Mahl'-tuh*], Lake. (E 1876) Named for the Malta Smelting Works, established after the Homestake Mine, nearby, started. Its purpose was to extract lead from the ore, most of which came from the Leadville area. The smelter may have taken its name from the island of Malta, at that time a British colony.

Manassa [*Muh-nas'uh*], Conejos. (E 1879; I 1899; P 814) When settled by Mormon colonists, Elder Lawrence M. Peterson suggested the name Manassa, in honor of the eldest son of Joseph, of ancient Israel. The town is noted as the home town of William Harrison (Jack) Dempsey, the "Manassa Mauler," world heavyweight boxing champion, 1919-26.

Mancos [*Mang'-kuhs*], Montezuma. (E 1881; I 1894; P 709) Named for the Mancos River, which, in Spanish, means "one-handed," "faulty," or "crippled."

Manitou Springs [*Man'-i-too*], El Paso. (E 1871; I 1888; P 4,278) First called Villa La Font (Fountain Village), the town was soon renamed Manitou, an Algonquin Indian word meaning "spirit." In 1935 the official name became Manitou Springs. This was the second time for such a change. In 1885 it became Manitou Springs but reverted to Manitou again in 1892. The site has always included many natural mineral springs.

Manzanola [*Man-zan-oh'-lah*], Otero. (E 1900; I 1900; P 451) The area was first settled in 1869 by two stockmen, Jasper M. and James W. Beaty, and a grocer, William H. May. Called Catlin, and incorporated under that name in 1891, it was reincorporated as Manzanola in 1900. The name, in Spanish, means "red apple," and is appropriate as the town is surrounded by orchards.

Marble, Gunnison. (E 1880 ?; I 1889; P 50) For the vast marble deposits along Yule Creek, south of the town. The Yule marble was used for the Lincoln Memorial and the Tomb of the Unknown Soldier in Washington, D.C. George Yule, an early pioneer, and for whom Yule Creek is named, also discovered the marble deposits high above the town.

Marshall, Boulder. (E 1878) One-time business center for a rich coal-mining territory. Founded by Joseph M. Marshall, who discovered coal, and for whom the mines and town were named. While the post office name was once changed to Langford (1882), probably for N.P. Langford, president of the Marshall Coal Co., the settlement continued to be known as Marshall.

Marvel, La Plata. (E 1915) Established on the homestead of John H. Miller, the family also having bought out , in the early 1900's, a grocery and general store. The name was taken from a cooperative flour mill named the Marvel Midget. (See: Kline, Colo.)

Masonville, Larimer. (E 1875) Once an important trading post, it was settled by Benjamin, James, and Joseph Miller, and named for James R. Mason, a rancher who laid out the site when gold was discovered nearby. When a post office was established in 1880, to avoid confusion with another Mason, postal authorities changed the name to Masonville.

Masters, Weld. (P.O. E 1900) Named by John Barton, owner of the 4-Bar Cattle Ranch, for his foreman, John Masters.

Matheson [*Math'-i-sun*], Elbert. (E 1886) For Duncan Matheson, early-day sheepman, upon whose land the town was built.

May Valley, Prowers. (E ca. 1904) Presumably for a settler's family name associated with a homesteader in the broad valley in which it lies. Lacking confirmation of any kind, the date is arbitrary and is based on the average settlement dates of nearby settlements.

Maybell, Moffat. (P.O. E 1884) The first post office in this vicinity was at Bell & Banks' ranch, and was named for Bell's wife, May.

Mayday, La Plata. (E 1890 ?) For the Mayday Mine established near Mayday Junction on the Rio Grande Southern Railroad.

McClave, Bent. (E 1906 ?) For B.T. McClave, owner of the townsite land. The settlement grew up around a beet dump of the American Beet Sugar Co. The town was established when the railroad was built into the area.

McCoy, Eagle. (E 1890) Settled and named by Charles H. McCoy, a rancher. McCoy was also the first postmaster when service was established in 1891.

Mead, Weld. (E 1905; I 1908; P 195) Dr. Martin S. Mead homesteaded here about 1886. In 1905 when the Great Western Sugar Co. built a spur and beet dump, Louis Roman and Paul Mead, son of the doctor, founded the town and named it in Dr. Mead's honor.

Meeker, Rio Blanco. (E 1882; I 1885; P 1,597) County seat. For Nathan C. Meeker, one of the founders of Greeley, Colo. While agent at the White River Ute Indian Agency in November, 1879, Meeker and agency employees were murdered by Indians; Meeker's wife and daughter and another woman carried away as captives. After the massacre, a military post called "Camp on White River" was established four miles above the ruined agency. It was abandoned in 1883, and all buildings sold to the residents of the valley, who thus acquired a ready-made town.

Meeker Park, Boulder. (E 1900 ?) Probably for nearby Mount Meeker, named for Nathan C. Meeker, a founder of Greeley, Colo. Also named for him is Meeker Ridge. (See: Meeker, Colo.)

Meredith, Pitkin. (E 1900) Named by A.E. Beard, apparently a town founder in some capacity, after a personal friend, in 1900.

Merino [*Muh-ree'-noh*], Logan. (E 1874; I 1917; P 260) Originally known as Buffalo, being settled by The Buffalo Colony. In 1882 the Union Pacific Railroad cut-off was being built and railroaders renamed the town for the huge flocks of Merino sheep raised in the community.

Mesa [*May'-suh*], Mesa. (E 1887 ?) For the Spanish word meaning "plateau" or "table land." The settlement grew on land homesteaded in 1887 in Plateau Valley by Archie R. Craig.

Mesita [*Muh-see'-tuh*], Costilla. (E 1909 ?) For the little flat-topped hill nearby. Mesita is a Spanish word meaning "small table land." The settlement was first called Hamburg, but was changed to avoid confusion with a similarly named town.

Milliken, Weld. (E 1909; I 1910; P 702) In honor of John D. Milliken, president of the Southwestern Land & Iron Co. He was also a founder of the Denver, Laramie & Northwestern Railroad.

Milner, Routt. (E 1917) Established as a supply point for the surrounding mining region by a pioneer banker and merchant named Milner (first name unknown).

Mineral Hot Springs, Saguache. (E 1880) Homesteaded in 1880 by Sylvester A. Jenks, the 37 medicinal springs were named in 1912 by Evertt Dunshee, whose father owned the site at that time.

Minturn [*Min'-tern*], Eagle. (E 1885; I 1904; P 706) For Thomas Minturn, a Denver & Rio Grande Western Railroad roadmaster.

Model, Las Animas. (E 1900 ?) First called Poso, Spanish for "dry hole," then Roby. The name was changed in 1920 when the community was intended to be a model town with its own irrigation district and platted townsite.

Moffat [*Mah'-fut*], Saguache. (E 1890; I 1911; P 98) Laid out by the San Luis Town & Improvement Assn. when the narrow-gauge Denver & Rio Grande Railroad was built into the region. The town was promoted by George H. Adams, S.N. Wood, Otto Mears, J.W. Gillully, and other railroad officials, and named for David H. Moffat, president of the railroad. At one time Moffat ranked first in Colorado as a stock loading center.

Molina [*Moh-lee'-nuh*], Mesa. (E 1883 ?) First known as Orson, for the postmaster, but when he, due to some difficulty, was asked to leave town, the office was renamed Snipes in honor of his successor. The present name, a Spanish word meaning "mill," came later after a water-power flour mill was built a short distance above the town on Cottonwood Creek.

Monte Vista [*Mont'-uh Vist'-uh*], Rio Grande. (E 1886; I 1886; P 3,909) A Spanish term meaning "mountain view." Prior to 1886, when it was formally platted and incorporated, the town was called Lariat, and later Henry.

Montezuma [*Mahn-ti-zoo'-muh*], Summit. (E 1865) For the last Aztec emperor of Mexico (1503-20). An early silver camp on a branch of the Snake River at the base of Glacier Mountain.

Montrose [*Mahnt-roz'*], Montrose. (E 1882; I 1882; P 6,496) County seat. Named by its founder, Joe Selig, and a great admirer of Sir Walter Scott, for the Dutchess of Montrose in Scott's *Legend of Montrose.*

Monument, El Paso. (E 1874; I 1881; P 393) For a rock formation to the west of the town. At the time of its founding there were two post offices in the county named Monument. In order to untangle the resultant mix-up, the name of Monument Station, given because of its proximity to Monument Park, was changed to Edgerton (it no longer exists). The other, called Henry Station by the Denver & Rio Grande Railroad, then adopted its post office name, Monument, as its official title.

Monument Park, Las Animas. (E 1927 ?) For Monument Lake in turn named for a natural stone obelisk rising from the waters. The lake was formed after a dam was constructed plus a resort area for the City of Trinidad.

Morrison, Jefferson. (E 1872; I 1906; P 429) For George Morrison, an 1859 pioneer, who homesteaded the townsite land.

Mosca [*Mohs'kuh*], Alamosa. (E 1890 ?) After Mosca Pass, which lies to the east. For a few years the town was known as Orean, but the name reverted to Mosca. Mosca Pass was named for Luis Di Moscasco, successor in command of De Soto's exploration party after De Soto's death in 1542.

Mount Crested Butte, Gunnison. (E 1974; I 1974; P est 200) For the nearby mountain, resembling a cock's comb. (See: Crested Butte, Colo.)

Mount Princeton Hot Springs, Chaffee. (E 1875 ?) Lying in the shadow of Mount Princeton (14,177 ft.) the town takes the name from the peak. The peak, in turn, one of the "Collegiate" peaks, is named for the eastern college.

Mountain View, Jefferson. (E 1904; I 1904; P 706) As the name implies, for the view of the Rocky Mountains to the west of the community.

Nathrop [*Nay'-throp*], Chaffee. (E 1880) The original town about a mile and a half above the present site, was known as Chalk Creek. It was one of the main stations on the stage line between Bale's Station and Leadville. It moved south in 1880 when the Denver & Rio Grande Railroad reached here. The site of the new settlement was owned jointly by Charles Nachtrieb, Denver, South Park & Pacific, and D&RG Railroads. The town was named for Nachtrieb—Nathrop being a corruption of his name—a pioneer merchant and freighter who crossed the plains in '59. He built the first grist mill in Lake County. He was murdered in Nathrop in 1881.

Naturita [*Nat-yoo-ree'-tuh*], Montrose. (E 1882; I 1951; P 820) Named after nearby Naturita Creek, a Spanish word, meaning "close to nature." The town was named by Rockood H. Blake, an early settler.

Nederland, Boulder. (E 1877; I 1885; P 492) Known as Brownsville in 1870, later as Middle Border, and still referred to as Tungsten Town. It was closely associated with the Caribou silver mines which were purchased by Dutch capitalists, who changed the name to Nederland prior to the filing of the site plat in 1877. Nederland means "low land," and was chosen because the Breed Mill (which cast the silver bricks President Grant walked upon at Central City in 1873), was built below the Caribou Mine. Caribou, now a ghost town to the west, was once a booming mining camp.

New Castle, Garfield. (E 1884; I 1890; P 499) Known as Grand Butte in 1866, and as Chapman in 1867. It was renamed by the Colorado Fuel & Iron Co. in 1888 after the discovery of large bituminous coal fields, for New Castle, famous mining center in England.

Ninaview [*Nigh'-nuh-vyoo*], Bent. (E 1915) When a post office was established, it was requested that the name Nina, honoring the wife of T.R. Jones on whose ranch the building stood, be used. Postal authorities added the word "view," thus forming the present name.

Niwot [*Nye'-watt*], Boulder. (E 1872) Founded by W.T. Wilson and first called Modoc. It was changed to Ni-Wot in 1879, for the nearby Ni-Wot mine and mill. Ni-wot is the Indian name for Left Hand Creek, honoring Left Hand, chief of a band of Arapaho Indians, who was esteemed by early settlers for his honesty and friendliness. The original Arapaho spelling and pronunciation was Nawat, later usage becoming Ni-Wot, and finally to its current spelling.

North Avondale, Pueblo. (P.O. E 1917) Probably for the Avon River in England, the word "north" to differentiate from the nearby town of Avondale. (See: Avondale, Colo.)

North Pole, El Paso. (E 1956) Santa's Workshop, North Pole, near the foot of Pikes Peak, is an attraction built to cater to children first, and adults second. The name is self-explanatory. It is a near duplication of a

North Pole built in upper New York in 1949. The original was designed by a Walt Disney artist, from ideas of a little girl telling how she thought Santa's home and workshop looked.

Northglenn, Adams. (E 1959; I 1969; P 27,937) A generic, soothing type of name without specific meaning. The developers later opened a shopping center area labeled Southglenn.

Norwood, San Miguel.(E 1885; I 1903; P 408) Named for a community in Missouri, by its founder, I.M. Copp.

Nucla [*New'-cluh*], Montrose. (E 1904; I 1915; P 949) Established by the Colorado Cooperative Co. as a socialistic colony. The name suggested by C.E. Williams is a corruption of nucleus, "a center." Chosen because the colonists believed the socialistic form of government would spread over the nation, and that their town would be the center of the movement.

Nunn [*Nun'*], Weld. (E 1904; I 1908; P 269) In honor of Tom Nunn, homesteader, who prevented a serious train wreck by flagging a train after he discovered a burning bridge near Pierce. As a token of its appreciation, the Union Pacific Railroad built a house for Nunn. About 1904, when a switch was built by the railroad, John Peterson, section foreman, suggested it be named for Nunn. The town previously had been known as Maynard, having been laid out by Murry & Bancroft of Denver.

Oak Creek, Routt. (E 1907; I 1907; P 492) Until its founding, the site of this coal mining town was ranch land, the homestead of Ernest Shuster. The Oak Creek Town, Land & Mining Co. founded the village and named it for the creek upon which it lies.

Ohio, Gunnison. (E 1880) For Ohio Creek, which flows through the town. Ohio is an Iroquois Indian word meaning "beautiful river." The community experienced two booms—early when minerals were first discovered in Colorado, and again in 1899, as the center of a gold-producing district. Previously known as Ohio City.

Olathe [*Oh-lay'-thuh*], Montrose. (E 1881; I 1907; P 756) First known as Brown, it was later called Colorow, a name by which the early settlers unwittingly honored a renegade Ute Indian Chief. When this fact became known, the Kansas emigrants changed it to Olathe, probably because they came from that Kansas town.

Olney Springs [*Awl'-nee*], Crowley. (E 1887; I 1912; P 264) Supposedly for a man named Olney, a representative of the Missouri Pacific Railroad when tracks were laid here. Reportedly named by daughter of railroad financier Jay Gould. (See: Haswell, Colo.)

Ophir [*Oh'-fer*], San Miguel. (E 1878; I 1881; P 6) For the Biblical reference to the location of King Solomon's mines, "the mines of Ophir."

Orchard, Morgan. (E 1890) The present town is about five miles distant from Fremont's Orchard, once-noted point on an immigrant trail. The "Orchard" was a large grove of stunted cottonwoods which, at a distance, appeared as an eastern apple orchard, and a welcome sight in staging days across treeless plains. The grove got its name because Col. John C. Fremont camped here on one of his exploring expeditions.

Orchard City, Delta. (E 1912; I 1912) For the orchards surrounding it—called the "fruit bowl" of Delta County.

Ordway, Crowley.(E 1890; I 1900; P 1,017) County seat. Founded on land taken up by George N. Ordway after he came west after the Civil War. The Ordway Town & Land Co. was organized by Ordway and the town named in his honor.

Otis, Washington. (E 1883; I 1917; P 521) No known reason, though the possibility exists it may honor someone connected with the Chicago Burlington & Quincy Railroad which pushed through the area about this time. For many years it was believed the name honored Dr. W.O. Otis, an early resident. Later research indicated Dr. Otis came to Colorado after the town was platted and named.

Ouray [*Oor'-aye*], Ouray. (E 1875; I 1884; P 741) County seat. For the famous Ute Indian Chief, Ouray. First a silver camp—and known as Uncompahgre or Uncompahgre City—it then languished until 1896 when gold was discovered by Thomas F. Walsh, who later became a bonanza king. (See: Camp Bird, Colo.)

Ovid [*Oh'-vid*], Sedgwick. (E 1908; I 1925; P 463) For many years a siding between Julesburg and Sedgwick, known only to railroad men. The section hands called the location Ovid for Newton Ovid, a bachelor who lived nearby, and the name later became official.

Oxford, La Plata (P.O. E 1904) Formerly called Grommet. Supposedly changed to its present name because it sounded better. One researcher has noted that many place names are commemorative of British toponymy—such as Oxford. The name Oxford was used starting in 1908.

Padroni [*Pad'-roan-ee*], Logan. (E 1909) This large sugar beet station was named for two Italian farmers in the vicinity, George and Tom Padroni. Until establishment of a reservoir in 1909, Padroni consisted only of a section house, built about 1899, when the Burlington Railroad came through the area.

Pagoda [*Puh-goh'-duh*], Routt. (E 1890) Founded by State Sen H. H. Eddy (1887-89), and named for nearby Pagoda Peak (11,257 ft.), so-called because it resembles an oriental pagoda.

Pagosa Junction [*Puh-goh'-suh*], Archuleta. (E 1899) A Ute Indian name meaning "healing waters." (See: Pagosa Springs, Colo.)

Pagosa Springs [*Puh-goh'-suh*], Archuleta. (E 1883; I 1891; P 1,360) County seat. This region was long occupied by prehistoric agricultural Indians. In later years the nomadic Utes found the medicinal waters beneficial. They made the springs a favorite camping place, and gave them the name Pagosah, "healing waters." The springs were first seen by whites in July, 1859, by the U.S. Topographical Engineers.

Palisade, Mesa. (E 1895; I 1904; P 874) First called Palisades, for the high perpendicular bluffs edging the valley on the north. The palisades served as a conserver of heat and a director of the air current, called the Million Dollar Breeze, which prevents the settling of frost in early spring when the vast orchards are in bloom.

Palmer Lake, El Paso. (E 1880; I 1889; P 947) Honoring Gen. William J. Palmer of Denver & Rio Grande Railroad fame. The lake around which the town is built was christened Palmero by Kate Field, noted lecturer, but the name was soon changed to Palmer. It was once known as Divide Lake and the original railroad station was also Divide. The post office called it Weissport, for C. A. Weiss, first station agent for D&RG. Dr. Finley Thompson, who settled in the area in 1882, had land surveyed and platted and established the town and was its first mayor.

Paoli [*Pay'-oh-lee*], Phillips. (E 1895; I 1930; P 52) For Paoli, Penn., and named by a chief engineer of the Chicago, Burlington & Quincy Railroad when the line came through here. The Pennsylvania town was named for an Italian general, Pasquale Paoli.

Paonia [*Pay'-own-ee-uh*], Delta. (E 1881; I 1902; P 1,161) Founded by Samuel Wade, rancher, who planted an orchard and established the first general store in the region. He secured a post office and suggested the name Peony (genus Peaonia), for a flower common to the region. Postal authorities saw fit to change it to Paonia.

(**Parachute,** Garfield.) Former name of Grand Valley. (See: Grand Valley.)

Paradox, Montrose. (E 1882 ?) The town and the creek on whose banks it lies, were named for Paradox Valley, so called because the Dolores River cuts through its cliff walls at right angles, an unusual phenomenon. Early settlers found the valley almost inaccessible, and had to unload their wagons, take them apart, and lower the pieces by ropes from a ledge to the floor of the valley.

Parkdale, Fremont. (E 1878 ?) Once known as Current Creek Station, it is believed by early settlers to have been named because the Arkansas Valley widens into park-like country here. The town was originally situated on the freight road to Silver Cliff and Leadville, and it was here that the Arkansas River was forded.

Parker, Douglas. (E 1870 ?) In early days this was a station of the stage line from Denver to Colorado Springs on the old Happy Canon Road. The post office was first called Pine Grove. Later changed to Parker for James S. Parker, who served 33 years as postmaster, and who in the early 1860's was a stage driver on the Smoky Hill route. In 1870 Parker bought the ranch that was the site of the station and post office.

Parlin, Gunnison. (E 1877) Settled by James Parlin, a dairy rancher. About 1880 officials of the now abandoned, narrow gauge South Park Railway wanted to buy 1,000 acres of land for a right-of-way and told Parlin to set his price. The old man in his goodness of heart is said to have replied, "You can have 1,500 acres free if you will put a depot over there by the dairy and make your trains stop for five minutes," this to permit the train crew and passengers to drink a glass of milk. Reportedly, the agreement was kept for a time.

Parshall, Grand. (E 1907) Settled by a Mr. Dow who set up a small store and circulated a petition for a post office. The name Parshall, honoring a pioneer of the region, was suggested. Postal authorities accepted it as there was no other office by this name in the country.

Peckham [*Peck'-um*], Weld. (E 1898) Early a side track on the Union Pacific Railroad, the town came into being when John Peckham opened a cheese factory here.

Peetz, Logan. (E 1889; I 1917; P 186) First named Mercer by the Burlington Railroad when a section house and depot were built here. Because the name was similar to a town in western Colorado, the settlement was renamed for Peter Peetz, a pioneer homesteader who lived nearby.

Penrose, Fremont. (E 1908) Established by the Beaver Park Land & Water Co., the town was named for Spencer Penrose, Colorado Springs capitalist and the company's largest stockholder. (See: Broadmoor, Colo.)

Peyton [*Pay'-tun*], El Paso. (E1888) Originally called Mayfield, the settlement was renamed in honor of George Peyton after the post office refused to honor the old name. Peyton was an original town settler.

Phippsburg, Routt. (E 1905) Established as a division point on the Denver & Salt Lake Railway—being halfway between Kremmling and Steamboat Springs. The name honors U.S. Sen. Lawrence C. Phipps (1925-31), because of his interest in the extension of the railroad.

Pierce, Weld. (E 1907; I 1918; P 452) Long before there was a settlement here, the Union Pacific Railroad built a switch and water tank on the site, calling it Pierce. The name honors Gen. John Pierce, former Surveyor General of Colorado Territory, and one-time president of the Denver Pacific Railroad. When the town was established by John E. and Bert A. Shafer, the name Pierce was retained.

Pine, Jefferson. (E 1882) While a post office was established under the name of Pine in 1882, the now-abandoned narrow-gauge railroad name for the settlement was Pine Grove. The stands of pine trees in the area suggested the name for this pioneer resort.

Pinecliffe, Boulder. (E 1900 ?) Named about 1900 by a Dr. Craig, a minister, for an unusually beautiful cliff nearby. The settlement was originally called Gato, a Spanish word meaning "wildcat."

Pinewood Springs, Larimer. (E 1903 ?) Originally known as Little Elk Park and changed about 1960 when a new development was underway. The name is a generic one—for the trees and natural springs.

Pitkin, Gunnison. (E 1879; I 1880; P 44) First known as Quartzville when the town was laid out, the name was changed the same year to honor Gov. F.W. Pitkin, a friend of the first postmaster, Frank Curtis.

Placerville [*Plass'-er-ville*], San Miguel. (E 1877 ?) Founded as a gold-mining town, and named for the placer mines in the vicinity. In 1909 the town was almost completely washed away by a flood. The site was abandoned and a new depot and business section built about half a mile up the San Miguel River. The settlement was first referred to as Dry Diggings and then Hangtown, prior to its present name.

Platoro [*Plat-or'-oh*], Conejos. (E 1882 ?) The name is Spanish, a combination of plata, "silver," and oro, "gold." Now a ghost camp, it reached its heyday in the late 1880s.

Platteville, Weld. (E 1871; I 1887; P 683) Founded when the Platte River Land Co. purchased several thousand acres in the valleys of the South Platte and St. Vrain Rivers, from the Denver Pacific Railway & Telegraph Co. A central location, on the east bank of the Platte River, was chosen for the town, which was named for the stream.

Pleasant View, Montezuma. (E 1941) For the pleasant vistas in the area. An earlier settlement, Ackmen, two or three miles to the southwest, started about 1913. When, in the 1930s, the road from Cortez to Dove Creek (now U.S. 666) was made a state highway, a new town was laid out on the newly aligned road and called Pleasant View. The Ackmen post office was closed and the new town absorbed the business interests.

Poncha Springs [*Pahn'-chah*], Chaffee. (E 1879; I 1880; P 198) Indians knew of the "great medicine waters" hot springs—99 in number—about three-quarters of a mile above town. The town was named for Poncha Pass, at whose foot it lies. Two explanations have been given. First is that Poncha is the misspelled form of pancho (Spanish for "paunch" or "belly") as descriptive of the low bend in the mountain range here. Second, that is an Indian word meaning tobacco, and was given for a weed that grew abundantly on the pass and which was an excellent substitute for tobacco.

Poudre Park [*Poo'-der Park*], Larimer. (E 1915) Homesteaded by Thomas H. Farrell and earlier called Columbine. The name is taken from the adjacent Cache la Poudre River, known locally as the Poudre. It refers to the cache of powder by employees of the American Fur Co. who buried supplies—including several kegs of gunpowder—near Laporte. The reason was to lighten the loads of their teams enroute to the Green River. Poudre is French for "powder."

Powder Wash, Moffat. (E 1931 ?) For Powder Wash Creek, possibly for powdery soil. A community of oil-field workers.

Powderhorn, Gunnison. (E 1876) This early health resort was founded as White Earth, near Cebolla Hot Springs. Two versions of the unusual name: One is that Cebolla Valley has the appearance of a huge powderhorn; the other is that one of the early white pioneers found a powderhorn on the creek flowing into the Cebolla.

Pritchett [*Prit'-chut*], Baca. (E 1920; I 1923; P 170) Marking the western terminus for a branch of the Atchison, Topeka & Santa Fe Railway, it was named for Dr. Henry S. Pritchett, one of the railroad's directors.

Proctor, Logan. (E 1908) J.D. Blue, of Cedar Rapids, Iowa, with several friends, purchased 5,000 acres—much of what was later known as the Blue Ranch—and laid out a townsite along the Union Pacific Railroad. The name was probably given to honor Redfield Proctor, President Benjamin Harrison's Secretary of War. Other references are to a "General" and "Captain" Proctor as an Indian fighter with Gen. George Crook.

Prospect Valley, Weld. (E 1922) Settled by a John G. Michael, and named for the Prospect Valley School, so called because the valley is one of the most fertile in the state.

Pryor, Huerfano. (E 1867) For Mack and Ike Pryor, who settled here just after the Civil War and went into the cattle business.

Pueblo [*Pweb'-low*], Pueblo. (E 1858; I 1885; P 97,453) County seat. Known first as Independence, the name was soon changed to Pueblo, Spanish for "town" or "village." The earlier name came about because a group from Indepencence, Mo., started a settlement west of one called Fountain, which was later absorbed into Pueblo. Pueblo had been a settlement for many years before, being occupied at intervals by Spaniards, trappers, Indian traders, and Mexicans. In 1806 Lt. Zebulon Pike erected a crude log cabin here, and Maj. Jacob Fowler, a trapper, built a log house here in 1822. By 1841 there was even an adobe fort.

Punkin Center, Lincoln. (E 1918 ?) Earlier called Prairie Dream, later Howard Stevens. When the present name was taken is uncertain but a Ralph Haddock said he used it for a sales tax registration in 1946. The name is a corruption of "pumpkin," and honored a resident who grew large pumpkins.

Purcell, Weld. (E 1910) Honoring Lawrence M. Purcell, upon whose land the town was located. When the Union Pacific Railroad built a stub line and a station, its name was Hungerford, for the superintendent of the Pullman Car Co.

Radium, Grand. (P.O. E 1906) The community was settled by Tim Mugrage and his family. The name was suggested by Harry S. Porter, prospector and miner, in 1906, because of the radium content in a mine he owned near the town.

Ramah [*Ray'-muh*], El Paso. (E 1888; I 1927; P 101) While it is reported the name was given by the El Paso Land & Water Co., who platted the town, no indication is given as to the meaning. Another report is that the wife of a Rock Island Railway official named the town. Supposedly she was reading a book as she came through on one of the first trains. As she had encountered the name Ramah in the story, she suggested it as the name for the settlement.

Rand, Jackson. (E 1881 ?) For a gruff and grizzled frontier scout trapper and early pioneer, Jack Rand. A post office was established in 1883.

Rangley [*Range'-lee*], Rio Blanco. (E 1885; I 1946; P 1,591) Settled as a trading post by Charles and Frank Hill and D. B. Case. Case named the settlement for Rangley, Mass.

Raymer, Weld. (E 1888; I 1919; P 68) While most of the district was vacated in 1893 and January, 1894, the site was again platted in 1909. The Lincoln Land Co. named the town Raymer, honoring George Raymer, an assistant chief engineer on the Burlington & Missouri

Railroad. Postal authorities called it New Raymer to avoid confusion with Ramah, Colo. (The Zip Code directory lists it as New Raymer, the State Highway map as Raymer.)

Raymond, Boulder. (E 1895 ?) For a family name and first called Raymond Ranch. Later called Raymonds (no apostrophe). It once was an overnight stopping place for travelers from Jimtown via Gresham to Allenspark and Estes Park.

Red Feather Lakes, Larimer. (E 1923) This resort town was founded by a Mr. Princell and named by him for Chief Redfeather, hero of a Cherokee Indian legend.

Red Mountain, Ouray. (E 1882 ?) First called Red Mountain City, and now a mining ghost town which burned in 1939. The name and that of the Red Mountain district came from three scarlet-hued peaks at whose feet they lie. Famous Otto Mears built a toll road from Silverton to Red Mountain, and later constructed a branch of the Denver & Rio Grande Railroad to the camp.

Red Wing, Huerfano. (E 1913) When the first store was built here, residents asked for a post office and requested the name Crestone. This was refused because of a town by that name in Saguache County. As a group of residents discussed the rejection, a Mexican came by whistling the tune "Red Wing." The name was sent to the post office and approved.

Redcliff, Eagle. (E 1879; I 1880; P 621) Remarkable discoveries of silver-lead carbonates on Battle Mountain attracted many miners. The nearest place with enough level ground was where the Eagle River Canyon broadens at its conjunction with Homestead and Turkey Creeks. The miners first called their settlement Cliff. Redcliff was named for the neighboring quartzite cliffs, and is often spelled as two words.

Redmesa [*Red-may'-suh*], La Plata. (E 1908) Established by Mormon settlers and first called Garland, the name was unsatisfactory because of another Garland in the state. At a group meeting, the settlers chose Red Mesa for the color of the soil and a nearby mesa. The name has evolved into one word.

Redstone, Pitkin. (E 1903) For the vivid red sandstone exposure nearby. Founded by the Colorado Fuel & Iron Co., it was built as a model industrial village.

Redvale, Montrose. (E 1908 ?) Originally called Redlands because of the reddish soil in the area. With the coming of the post office, the name was changed to Redvale to avoid confusion with Redlands, Calif.

Rico [*Ree'-coh*], Dolores. (E 1879; I 1880; P 275) County seat. After Col. J.C. Haggerty's discovery of silver in 1879, a rush of prospectors poured into the district because the ore was so rich. Variously called Carbon City, Carbonville, Lead City, and Dolores City, a meeting was finally called to choose a name. William Weston, then of Ouray, suggested the Spanish word Rico ("Rich"), which was adopted.

Ridgway, Ouray. (E 1890; I 1891; P 262) Named for R.M. Ridgway, superintendent of the Mountain Division of the Denver & Rio Grande Railroad. Early it was a forwarding point for wagon transportation to the mines.

Rifle, Garfield. (E 1882; I 1905; P 2,150) About 1880 several soldiers were working on the road between Meeker and the present site of Rifle, placing mile-posts between the Colorado and White Rivers. One of the men left his rifle at a night camp. When he discovered his loss, he returned for it, and found it on the bank of a stream, which was immediately dubbed Rifle Creek. When the settlement was founded, it took its name from the stream.

Rio Blanco [*Ree-oh Blahng'-koh*], Rio Blanco. (E 1899) From the Spanish, meaning "White River." It was formerly spelled as one word: Rioblanco.

River Bend, Elbert. (E 1870) One of the older settlements in eastern Colorado, on Big Sandy Creek, upon whose banks the Sand Creek Massacre of 1864 occurred. In 1870 it was the terminus of the Kansas Pacific Railroad. The town's name comes from its location on a bend in the Big Sandy River. (See: Chivington, Colo.)

Rockport, Weld. (E 1926) Built on land owned by Clark Coleman and named by Coleman for Rockport, Ill., where he probably once lived. However, the first building was of rocks, gathered in the area. Arthur DePorter, still living in the vicinity, helped Coleman haul the stones. Coleman started a garage and a lunchroom.

Rockvale, Fremont. (E 1882; I 1886; P 359) When the Santa Fe Railway proposed that a settlement be named for the former owner of the land, B.F. Rockafellow, he objected. His wish, which was carried out, was that it be named for Rockvale, Md. It was, he said, "a beautiful valley bound in by rocky walls." Rockafellow's regiment had camped there during the Civil War.

Rockwood, La Plata. (E 1878) Two possibilities exist for the town's name. Thomas Rockwood, a pioneer of the region, thought the town might have been named for him. It has also been said that the nearby stone quarries and timber stands suggested the name.

Rocky Ford, Otero. (E 1870; I 1887; P 4,859) Two towns of this name were founded. The first was on the Arkansas River, 20 miles above Fort Bent, at a ford used in time of high water by freighters and cattle drives. A post office was established and a small settlement grew. When the Santa Fe Railway was extended to Pueblo, the post office and store moved from the old town to the site of the present city, about three miles to the southwest. The name comes from the gravel-lined ford across the river.

Roggen, Weld. (E 1883 ?) First known as Blair, but changed by the post office because of a Blair, Neb. The name Roggen was given by postal authorities, but the source is controversial. One version is that it was named for one of the surveyors of the Burlington & Missouri Railroad. Another version is that the name honors Edward P. Roggin, a former Nebraska Secretary of State.

Rollinsville, Gilpin. (E 1861 ?) Founded by John Q.A. Rollins, and named in his honor. The early mining camp was unique in that saloons, gambling houses, and dance halls were not allowed. The settlement was the starting point of a wagon road constructed by Rollins over the Continental Divide—called Rollins Pass—and on into Hot Sulphur Springs and Middle Park.

Romeo, Conejos. (E 1899; I 1923; P 352) First a siding of the Denver & Rio Grande Railroad for the convenience of the small community and nearby Manassa. A signboard bore the name Sunflower and a post office of that name was established at a ranch house. A plat was filed in 1899 by the Romero Town Co. The name Romero honored an early settler. However, confusion was caused by another town also bearing this name, and the Conejos town was changed to Romeo.

Rosedale, Weld. (E 1939; I 1939; P 80) Platted as a 40-acre settlement on Greeley's south border, to circumvent "dry" laws of that city. (Greeley was a "temperance" town until 1969.) At one time the nickname "Boozeville" was applied. The original plat was filed by George E. Kenrick and his wife, Rose Agnes Kendrick. The name would seem to stem from her first name.

Rosita [*Roh-zee'-tuh*], Custer. (E 1870) Richard Irwin, prospector and writer, established a camp here which developed into a settlement. It soon became known as Rosita (Spanish for "small rose").

Royal Gorge, Fremont. (E 1929) For the Royal Gorge of the Arkansas River. By Congressional action, in 1906 a 2,000-acre park was created along the rim of the spectacular gorge. In 1929 a suspension bridge was constructed across the gorge. Since then a cable car ride takes visitors to the floor of the defile, and an aerial tramway travels across the chasm.

There is no community as such except for the facilities for operating the attractions. A post office was opened in 1949.

Rush, El Paso. (E 1907) For Christopher (Chris) Rush, a homesteader who came to Colorado from Missouri, and settled here in 1907.

Rustic, Larimer. (E 1882) Established with the Rustic Hotel built by S.B. Stewart at the foot of Pingree Hill. Old timers termed a stay in the mountain as "rusticating," and "rustic" means a respite from ordinary demands. Teddy Roosevelt and U.S. Grant are said to have been among the rusticators.

Rye, Pueblo. (E 1882; I 1937; P 207) For the grain which surrounded the town. The first post office was established at the ranch of David Nichols, and was known as Table Mountain. Because postal authorities objected to the lengthy name, it was changed to Rye sometime before 1885.

Saguache [*Suh-watch'*], Saguache. (E 1867; I 1891; P 642) County seat. An early favorite site for Ute Indian encampments, and later a "resort" for fur traders and trappers from New Mexico. The latter could not pronounce the Indian name, Sa-gua-gua-chippa ("blue earth" or "water of the blue earth"), referring to a large spring in which blue clay was found. They abridged it to Saguache (Si-watch). Otto Mears, John Lawrence, and other associates started the settlement in 1867.

St. Elmo, Chaffee. (E 1880) Because it was necessary to cut down a heavy growth of pine and spruce trees before the town could be built, it was called Forest City. Postal authorities refused the name because of a conflict with a Forest City in California. Griffith Evans, first store operator, had recently read the novel *Saint Elmo*, and suggested the title for the town. While it once boasted a population of over 500, with the closing of the last mine in 1922 it became a ghost town.

Salida [*Suh-ligh'-duh*], Chaffee. (E 1880; I 1891; P 4,355) County seat. Originally known as South Arkansas, the town was founded by the Denver & Rio Grande Railroad when it reached here in 1880. The post office ordered the name changed in 1881. The new name was suggested by Gov. A.C. Hunt, an official of the railroad, who had recently visited Mexico. Salida in Spanish means "departure" or "outlet." In Mexico and other Spanish-speaking countries, the exit of a public building is labeled "Salida."

San Acacio [*San Uh-kash'-ee-oh*], Costilla. (E 1853) For Saint Acacius, a Spanish soldier who was cannonized. The first settlers here fought Indians in the name of San Acacio, and later named their post office for him.

San Francisco, Costilla. (E 1854) Settled as a Spanish community and probably named for an army man, Col. John Francisco.

San Luis [*San Loo'-is*], Costilla. (E 1851; I 1968; P 781) County seat. Known as the oldest town in Colorado, the original site being three-fourths of a mile below the present one. It was on the Sangre de Cristo Land Grant, given to Luis Lee and Narciso Beaubien in December, 1843. For many years it was known as Culebra or San Luis de Culebra, and as Plaza Del Medio (center village); while San Pedro, three miles above, was called Upper Culebra or Plaza Arriba; and San Acacio, three miles below, was Lower Culebra or Plaza Abajo. San Luis is Spanish for Saint Louis, patron saint.

San Pablo [*San Pab'-loh*], Costilla. (E 1851) Spanish for Saint Paul. In what was originally the Sangre de Cristo land grant which included, in Colorado, what is now Costilla County. The community of San Pedro (Spanish: Saint Peter) is sometimes said to have been on the same site earlier. But it would seem this has always been a separate community also settled in 1851.

Sanford, Conejos. (E 1881 ?; I 1907; P 638) Started as a Mormon settlement and named for Silas Sanford Smith, first president of the San Luis Stake. Earlier it was named Ephraim, younger son of Joseph of Israel in the Bible. Most of the early settlers were of Danish or English nationality.

Sapinero [*Sap-i-nehr'-oh*], Gunnison. (E 1888) Named in honor of Sapinero, a sub-chief of the Ute Indians, and a brother-in-law of the noted Chief Ouray. (See: Ouray, Colo.)

Sargents, Saguache. (E 1879 ?) For Joseph Sargent, once connected with the Los Pinos Indian Agency, who established a ranch here in 1879. In 1880 the ranch became a town and a post office was named Marshalltown, with Joseph Sargent as postmaster. The name of the settlement was changed to Sargents in 1882.

Saw Pit, San Miguel. (E 1895 ?; I 1896; P 26) Descriptive of the saw pits built to saw lumber by hand. A pit in the ground was used by a two-man crew. A log was placed over the pit, and with a huge saw, one man worked topside, the other in the pit, to rip out planks.

Security-Widefield, El Paso. (E 1955) Established as a new community by American Builders, headed by Fred Sproul, Security is apparently a "safe-sounding" name. In 1968 Jules Watson started a development called Widefield Homes, the name reflecting the open space concept.

Sedalia [*Si-dayl'yah*], Douglas. (E 1865) John H. Craig, who settled in Happy Canon in 1859, founded the present town of Sedalia as the Round

Corral in 1865. In 1870 it was sold and became Plum Station or the Town of Plum, because of East and West Plum Creeks. Later one of the original settlers, a native of Sedalia, Mo., changed the name to its present one.

Sedgwick, Sedgwick. (E 1887; I 1918; P 208) For historic old Fort Sedgwick, which is a few miles east of the town. The fort was named to honor Maj. Gen. John Sedgwick, a Union officer killed in 1864 at the battle of Spotsylvania Court House, in Virginia. The fort had had other names before it honored the Civil War officer in 1865.

Segundo [*Si-guhn'-doh*], Las Animas. (E 1901 ?) When the Colorado Fuel & Iron Co. bought large holdings in this region and began coal production, it named each coal mine and camp by number as it was opened. Segundo (Spanish for "second"), was the second camp founded.

Seibert [*See'-bert*], Kit Carson. (E 1888; I 1917; P 192) For Henry Seibert, New York City millionaire and an official of the Rock Island Railroad when the line built through here in 1888. Seibert (pronounced Si-bert but better known as See-bert), donated a library of 500 books to the town.

Severance, Weld. (E 1910; I 1920; P 59) For Dave Severance, who sold 160 acres of land to the Denver-Larimer Townsite Co., at a then astronomical price of $325 an acre.

Shaffers Crossing [*Shay'-furs*], Jefferson. (E 1865?) For pioneer settler Samuel Shaffer, on whose land the community started. Once a stop on stage lines from Denver to South Park and Leadville. Not listed on the official state map index, it is on U.S. 285 about midway between Conifer and Bailey. A county road leads to Deckers on the South Platte River. Map coordinates: G-13.

Shawnee, Park. (E 1878 ?) Named for nearby Shawnee Peak (12,400 ft.) by the Colorado & Southern Railway when it built through here in 1880. The name honors the Shawnee Indian tribe. The name is derived from "shawun," meaning "southerly," the tribe's correct name being Shawunogi, or "southerners." Originally the tribe came from South Carolina and Tennessee. Earlier names of the settlement were Fairville and Slaghts.

Sheridan, Arapahoe. (E 1887; I 1890; P 4,787) For Gen. Phil Sheridan of Civil War fame. The incorporation included the settlements of Sheridan Park, Military Park, Logantown, and Petersburg. The town is adjacent to the old Fort Logan military post. Petersburg (a name which lasted unofficially for many years) was adopted in honor of Peter Magnes, who had been known as "the father of the sugar beet industry."

Sheridan Lake, Kiowa. (E 1887; I 1951; P 86) Founded by the Sheridan Town Co. for Gen Phil Sheridan.

Silt, Garfield. (E 1908; I 1915; P 434) Founded by Henry Halsey, townsite owner, and originally called Ferguson. The settlement was renamed by the Denver & Rio Grande Western Railroad because of the nature of the soil.

Silver Cliff, Custer. (E 1878; I 1879; P 126) Since the time of the Pikes Peak gold rush, a low, black-stained cliff near here had attracted the attention of prospectors. In 1877 silver deposits were discovered here and soon the rich Horn Silver, Racine Boy, and Silver Cliff mines were established. When the rush was on to the Wet Mountain Valley, the growing town (which once aspired to be the state capital) took the name Silver Cliff.

Silver Plume, Clear Creek. (E 1870; I 1880; P 164) One version is that it honors a national political figure, James G. Blaine, who was known as the "Plumed Knight." Another is that the name was first applied to a mine in the district as the white streaks of silver appeared plume-like in the rocks.

Silverthorne, Summit. (E 1962; I 1967; P 400) For Marshall Silverthorn, who settled in Breckenridge, Colo., in 1860. He founded a hotel in the town which became famous in the area. The building was a historic landmark for almost a century, being razed in 1957. The town which commemorates Silverthorn's name ends with an "e." While the correct spelling seems to be without the final "e," some early accounts used it.

Silverton, San Juan. (E 1874; I 1885; P 797) County seat. Prior to the present settlement the first "community" on the site was known as Bakers Park. Prior to an election in 1875, when the name Silverton was chosen (signifying its place in the San Juan mining region), several other names were used, including Reeseville, Quito, and Greenville.

Simla [*Sim'-luh*], Elbert. (E 1888; I 1913; P 460) For years the railroad siding here had been known as Simla. The source of the name is nearly identical to that of Ramah. The daughter of a railroad official suggested the name because it occurred in a book she was reading when her father noticed the siding from a train. The town took its name from the siding.

Skyway, Mesa. (P.O. E 1927) This summer resort on Grand Mesa, was named in honor of the Skyway Drive over the mountain. At an elevation of 10,100 ft. the community once had one of the highest post offices in Colorado.

Slater [*Slay'-ter*], Moffat. (E 1876) Settled by William Slater, a trapper, and named in his honor.

Slick Rock, San Miguel (E 1879) First known as Snyder's Camp for a cattle camp. The name comes from a sandstone that is smooth and free of fractures. Geologists named it entrada sandstone. A radium mill was built here about 1905 but later closed.

Snowmass, Pitkin. (E 1889) For Snowmass Creek, on which it borders, and not for Snowmass Mountain (14,077 ft.), from which the stream gets its name.

Snowmass-at-Aspen, Pitkin. (E 1967) Established as a new ski resort, the name comes from its proximity to Aspen, and it, too, borders on Snowmass Creek and takes its water from East Snowmass Creek. It is now generally known as Snowmass Resort, but the official mailing address is West Village, Colo.

Snyder, Morgan. (E 1882) For J.W. Snyder, a pioneer cattleman.

Somerset, Gunnison. (E 1902) After the coal fields of the North Fork Valley were opened, the Denver & Rio Grande Railroad established the town and named it for a coal mining community in Pennsylvania.

South Fork, Rio Grande. (E 1880 ?) An early stage station, named for its location at the confluence of the South Fork of the Rio Grande del Norte with that of the main stream.

Spar City, Mineral. (E 1892) Founded as Fisher City after one of the discoverers of gold in the area. Name later changed to Spar City. Probably for the Big Spar mine nearby. Spar is a Cornish name for quartz and the area abounds in the rock. The town boomed and burst with the post office being discontinued in 1896. Today it is a ghost town.

Springfield, Baca. (E 1887; I 1889; P 1,660) County seat. The townsite promoters came from Winfield, Kan., and purchased the tract from Andrew Harrison, a native of Springfield, Mo. The new town was given the name of his home town.

Starkville, Las Animas. (E 1879; I 1954; P 166) The first coal mine operated near Trinidad was opened about 1879 by H.G. Stark, and was known as the Starkville Mine. The settlement, originally called San Pedro, was renamed in May, 1879, in honor of Stark.

State Bridge, Eagle. (E 1889) The large-span bridge across the Colorado River was the first state-financed bridge on the western slope. The name State Bridge was a logical one, and the name was used for the stage stop. Construction of the bridge was from 1889-91. Nearby is Rainbow Mountain, named for its many-hued rock formations.

Steamboat Springs, Routt. (E 1875; I 1907; P 2,340) County seat. The name is derived from the peculiar puffing sounds formerly emitted by one of the springs, resembling large river steamers in action. This spring was destroyed during the construction of the Moffat Railroad (now the Denver & Rio Grande Western) in 1908.

Sterling, Logan. (E 1873; I 1884; P 10,636) County seat. A railroad surveyor, David Leavitt, while in the area, liked the country so much he returned, started a ranch, and surveyed the Sterling Ditch. A post office was established on his ranch in 1872 called Sterling, for his home town in Illinois. With the coming of the Julesburg-Denver branch of the Union Pacific Railroad, the present town came into existence. The older settlement (about four miles west) was moved to the new townsite.

Stoneham, Weld. (E 1888) Derived from the family name of an early settler, Stone, combined with the first letters of the word "hamlet." The original community, about 2½ miles northwest of the present site, was destroyed by fire. The new Stoneham started to build about 1910.

Stoner, Montezuma. (E 1890 ?) Probably for the creek upon which it lies. The stream has been known as Stoner Creek by residents in the area since 1888.

Stonewall, Las Animas. (E 1867) The first resident was Juan Guitterez, who built a cabin here in 1867 and began grazing cattle. The valley, for a time, was known, in Spanish, as "El Valle del Guitterez." A James Stoner homesteaded somewhat to the west. Because of a rock formation on his place, the region was known as Stoner's wall. When the settlement needed a post office, in 1878, the name became Stonewall.

Stoneton, Baca. (E 1887) Name taken from a nearby stream which had many rocks and stones.

Strasburg [*Strahs'berg*], Arapahoe. (E 1890) For John Strasburg, who built a section of the track for the Union Pacific Railroad. The site of the town was homesteaded by D. H. Weaver, who laid it out in lots, built the first store, and served as the first postmaster.

Stratton, Kit Carson. (E 1888; I 1915; P 790) First known as Claremont. Named for Winfield Scott Stratton, Colorado Springs carpenter who became a mining magnate, with rich strikes in Cripple Creek. Town supposedly named for him in hopes he would donate money to the town. While he did spend some time in the community, there is no record he gave funds.

Sugar City, Crowley. (E 1891; I 1900; P 307) Founded by employees of the National Sugar Co., it takes its name for the large sugar factory established in the rich sugar beet region.

Summitville, Rio Grande. (E 1872) Probably because of its altitude—11,300 ft.—near the crest of the Continental Divide. Founded as a gold mining town. Also once known as Summit.

Sunbeam, Moffat. (E 1912) When the post office was established, N.C. Bonivee, a farmer, suggested the name because, he is quoted, the sun seemed to shine more brightly on this particular spot than anywhere else in the valley.

Superior, Boulder. (E 1897; I 1904; P 171) Probably for Superior, Wis., though another version is that a "Mr. Hake," who owned a coal mine, named it for a Nebraska town he liked.

Swink, Otero. (E 1900; I 1900; P 381) For State Sen. George W. Swink (1893-97) a farmer as well as legislator. Prior to the building of the Holly Sugar Co. factory, there had been a railroad stopping point, with a box car serving as a station, known as Fairmont.

Tabernash [*Tab'-er-nash*], Grand. (E 1905) Located on the old Junction Ranch, homestead of Edward J. Vulgamott, an 1882 pioneer. The ranch was named for its location at the junction of Rollins Pass and Berthoud Pass roads, and was a popular stopping place. Here a Ute Indian, Tabernash, was killed by a white man named "Big Frank," in 1879; the killing was a forerunner of the Meeker and Thornburg massacres. The town's impetus came with the building of the Denver & Salt Lake Railroad in 1902. E.A. Meredith, chief engineer, named it for the murdered Indian.

Teds Place, Larimer. (E 1922) Established by Edward Irving Herring—better known as Ted—when he returned from World War I. A landmark for tourists going to Poudre Canyon, as it marks the canyon's entrance.

Telluride [*Tel'-yoo-righd*], San Miguel. (E 1878; I 1887; P 553) County seat. Founded as Columbia, its growth was slow until the Denver & Rio Grande Southern Railroad was completed in 1890. The name was changed to Telluride, which is derived because of the tellurium ore found in the vicinity. Tellurium is a rare element analogous to sulphur, usually combined with metals—as gold and silver.

Texas Creek, Fremont. (E 1879 ?) Named for nearby Texas Creek. In pioneer times a Joseph Lamb and a companion drove a herd of Texas steers north to feed the miners. During an overnight stop a prowling bear stampeded the herd and the men were several days rounding it up. Lamb named the stream on which they camped Texas Creek.

Thatcher, Las Animas. (E 1880 ?) Originally a stage-station known as Hole-in-the-Rock, because of a natural spring where the stage horses were watered. The name was changed after several years to honor M.D. Thatcher, pioneer banker and businessman of southeastern Colorado.

The Forks. Larimer. (E 1875) For its location on Highway 287 where the road forks, toward Livermore. Started by Robert O. Roberts as a hotel for lumberjacks working in the area. It was also a stage-stop on the Denver-Laramie route. No longer a hotel, a restaurant is still maintained.

Thornton, Adams. (E 1952; I 1956; P 13,326) Named to honor Gov. Dan Thornton who was in office at the time the community was established.

Timnath [*Tim'-nath*], Larimer. (E 1882; I 1920; P 177) Established soon after the building of the Greeley, Salt Lake & Pacific Railroad, but apparently a nameless village. Twenty years later, when the Presbyterian Church was organized, the Rev. Charles A. Taylor, the first minister, named it Timnath. The 14th chapter of Judges in Holy Writ states, "And Samson went down to Timnath," a Philistine city where he saw a woman he later married.

Timpas [*Tim'-puhs*], Otero. (E 1868) For Timpas Creek, an Arkansas River tributary. Timpas is from the Spanish for timpa stone. A tymp stone is used in the front of the hearth of a blast furnace. There is a similar Latin definition. The creek's name appears on region maps of the early 1800's. It has been suggested limestone from the area might have been used at the old Bents Fort.

Tincup, Gunnison. (E 1879) Prospectors in 1861 found indications of gold in a dry wash. One of the men carried some dirt back to camp in a little tin cup he had attached to his belt. The sample proved rich in gold and the incident gave the names to Tin Cup Gulch, Tin Cup District, and finally to Tin Cup Camp. The town was once one of the largest and richest in the county. Except for summer residents, the town is deserted. For a brief period it also had the name of Virginia City.

Tiny Town, Jefferson. (E 1915) An elaborate miniature city built on the banks of Turkey Creek and named "Tiny Town" by George E. Turner. Turner came to Colorado at the age of six. He owned a Denver moving company ("The World Moves, So Does Turner" was his slogan) when he constructed the small structures—averaging 3 ft. in height. A resort village grew up around the small-scale community and retained the Tiny Town name.

Tobe [*towb*], Las Animas (P.O. E 1910) For Tobe Benavides, a local resident. When his name was submitted as the name for the settlement, the post office chose his first rather than last name for the town.

Toonerville Bent. (E 1928) Originally known as Red Rock, the community decided to adopt a new and unique name. It was suggested there might soon be a street car line to accommodate visitors, so the title Toonerville was adopted. The original Toonerville was a mythical town in the nationally syndicated cartoon created by Fontaine Fox titled "Toonerville Folks."

Toponas [*Top'-ohn-us*], Routt (E 1888) For the Indian word "Toponas" meaning "sleeping lion" or "panther" and given because a nearby hill resembles, from a distance, a recumbent lion with head erect.

Towaoc [*Toy'-yawk*], Montezuma. (E 1920) A Ute Indian word meaning "all right." When they first moved the Ute Mountain Sub-agency here from Navajo Springs, three miles north, they thought it was "Towaoc." The word is a substitute for "thank you," for which they do not have a phrase. The contract to build the new agency actually was let in 1916, but took four years to complete. A post office, then and now, is in the Trading Post. The Navajo Springs post office was established in 1910.

Towner, Kiowa. (E 1887-?) Founded by the Missouri Pacific Railroad and named for a railroad official. Earlier, the community was known as Memphis. The town is known for the Towner bus tragedy of March, 1931. A school bus with 22 children was caught in a blizzard. The driver perished trying to get help. One of the pupils, Bryan Unteidt, helped keep most of the children alive by compelling them to exercise and play games. In recognition of his heroism, Bryan was publicly honored by President Herbert Hoover at the White House.

Trinchera, Las Animas. (E 1873 ?) The name is a Spanish word meaning "trench" or "entrenchment" and given the village because of a gap or pass opening through a nearby mesa. Earlier it was known as San Jose, and later Grinell.

Trinidad [*Trin'-i-dad*], Las Animas. (E 1859; 1879; P 9,901) County seat. Long a favorite rendezvous with early trappers, traders, and travelers with a permanent settlement starting in 1859. The name given originally was "Santisima Trinidad," ("most holy trinity"), later shortened to the present name. Its first name, when the first cabin was built by Gabriel and Juan N. Guiterrrez, was Rio de Las Animas.

Twin Lakes, Lake (E 1880 ?) For the two natural lakes, each about two miles in width and five miles in length, which give the community its name. Settlement was made after the Leadville silver rush. The town is at the foot of Colorado's hightest peak, Mount Elbert (14,431 ft.).

Two Buttes, Baca. (E 1909; I 1911; P 138) Named by the Two Buttes Townsite Co. because of its proximity to striking buttes near the Baca and Prowers County line, about 13 miles north of the town. It was the first incorporated town in the county.

Tyrone [*Tuh-rohn'*], Las Animas. (P.O. E 1916) Founded as Yetta and changed to Tyrone in 1929. No official reason is given for the name, though it possibly is for a landowner or pioneer resident. Tyrone is a county in Ireland whose name has been used in this country—in Pennsylvania, for example.

Uravan [*Orr'-uh-van*], Montrose. (E 1912-?) Named in 1936 when the United States Vanadium Corp. began work here. Uravan is an acronym—first syllables of uranium and vanadium, minerals occurring with carnotite. Carnotite was first mined here in 1881 for the small amounts of gold found in it. In 1898 the Smithsonian Institution found the ore contained uranium and several tons of ore were shipped to France. Madam Curie used this ore in her experiments that resulted in the extraction of radium. Up to 1928, ores taken from this area accounted for almost half of the world's production of radium.

Utleyville [*Ut'-lee-vil*], Baca. (E 1918) Settled by a family named Utley. The post office was opened in 1918, with A. H. Utley as postmaster.

Vail, Eagle. (E 1959; I 1966; P 484) For nearby Vail Pass (10,603 ft.) which was, in turn, named for Charles D. Vail, Colorado State Highway Engineer in the 1930s.

Vancorum, Montrose. (E 1930) Established only as a "housing development" by and for the Vanadium Corporation of America. The name is an acronym using the first letters of the corporate name. Somewhere during the years, however, the "am" became "um" on the map. The community had houses only, no store, church, or postoffice.

Vernon, Yuma. (E 1892) Formerly called Condon's Corners, for Barney Condon, founder of the *Wray Rattler* newspaper (1886-1948). He homesteaded and had a small store west of the present town in 1880. When the site was laid out in 1892 by a townsite committee, each member proposed a name. T. A. Wilson's suggestion was agreed upon—but no record indicates what the name means. One thought is commemorating George Washington's home, Mount Vernon.

Victor, Teller. (E 1893; I 1894; P 258) Early known as The City of Mines for its great gold producing district (along with nearby Cripple Creek).

Named partly for the Victor Mine and because of its nearness to the larger producing mines. Boyhood home of writer-broadcaster Lowell Thomas.

Vilas [*Vigh'-lus*], Baca. (E 1888; I 1888; P 83) For William F. Vilas of Wisconsin, Secretary of the Interior in President Grover Cleveland's cabinet 1888-1889. Prior to this he was Postmaster General, and it could be it was for this honor the community was named for him. From 1891-97 he was a Senator for Wisconsin.

Villa Grove [*Vil-lah- Grove'*], Saguache. (E 1870) For the Italian word villa ("village") because a beautiful grove surrounded the original townsite. Until the extension of the Denver & Rio Grande Railroad down the San Luis Valley to Alamosa in 1890, it was the terminus of a narrow-gauge branch from Poncha Pass. First known as Garibaldi the name was changed in 1872 to Villagrove and later to the present two-word spelling.

Villegreen [*Vil-lah-Green'*], Las Animas. (E 1917) A name coined by the post office when a list of possible names, submitted by the community's residents was rejected. The Postal authorities combined the French word for "village" with J. L. Greene's surname. The suggestion, Villegreen, was accepted by the town. Greene was named first postmaster.

Vineland, Pueblo. (E 1876) For early vineyards in the area. These gradually disappeared as general farming and ranching became predominant.

Virginia Dale, Larimer. (E 1862) A favorite camping place for emigrant trains from 1864-66. The present community was built around a bullet-scarred stage station, established in 1862 by Joseph A. (Jack) Slade. It was named by him for his wife, Virginia Dale.

Vona, Kit Carson. (E 1888; I 1919; P 114) First settled mainly by employees of the Rock Island Railroad. The town was promoted by Pearl S. King, an attorney of Burlington, Colo. and named for his niece, Vona.

Wagon Wheel Gap, Mineral. (E 1872 ?) An early stage station on the route to Lake City in the early 1870s. There were mineral springs here and the Hot Springs Hotel was built in 1877. The name is derived from a large wagon wheel found here, supposed to have been left by the Baker prospecting party of 1861, on their way out of the mountains. It was thereafter spoken of as the gap where the wagon wheel was found.

Walden, Jackson. (E 1889; I 1890; P 907) County seat. Once known as Sagebrush. The present name honors Mark A. Walden, one time postmaster at now-ghost town Sage Hen Springs, about four miles southwest.

Walsenburg, Huerfano. (E 1873; I 1873; P 4,329) County seat. Started as a little Mexican settlement known as La Plaza de los Leones, for Don Miguel Antonio Leon, an early settler. In 1870, Fred Walsen opened a general store and became a community leader. When the village was incorporated it was changed in his honor. In 1887 postal authorities changed the name to Tourist City, but indignant citizens demanded the return of the old name.

Walsh, Baca. (E 1914; 1928; P 989) For a retired general baggage agent for the Atchison, Topeka, & Santa Fe Railway.

Ward, Boulder. (E 1865; I 1896; P 32) For Calvin W. Ward, who discovered, in 1860, the gold-bearing seam known as the Ward Lode. The now-abandoned Denver, Boulder & Western Railroad (the "Switzerland Trail of America"), made daily runs to Ward, the first of the camps in the iron-copper-sulphide belt.

Waterton, Jefferson. A community of residences for employees of the Denver Water Board at the Kassler Filter Plant. While the Waterton name remains, it bears the name Kassler on the state map and index. (See: Kassler, Colo.)

Watkins, Adams. (E 1872) Established by the Kansas Pacific Railroad (now part of the Union Pacific system), it was first called Box Elder. Later it was re-named for L. A. Watkins, a local rancher and merchant.

Waunita Hot Springs [*Wahn-ee'-tuh*], Gunnison. (E 1884) When the medicinal springs—some 200—were purchased in 1884 by Dr. Charles G. Davis of Chicago, he changed the name from Tomichi Hot Springs (it lies at the foot of Tomichi Dome, 11,384 ft.), to Waunita Hot Springs. During World War I it was found the springs contained permanent activity and a strong emenation of radium. Dr. Davis then renamed the place Waunita Hot Radium Springs. Several years ago the name was changed to its present form. No record shows where the name Waunita came from; possibly a Davis family member.

Weldona [*Wel-doh'-nuh*], Morgan. (E 1866) For either a resident or an Army general named Weldon. Later it was known as Deuel but changed to Weldona. The letter "a" was added to reduce confusion with the town of Walden.

Wellington, Larimer. (E 1902; I 1905; P 691) Named for a Traffic Manager of the Colorado & Southern Railway whose name was Wellington.

Westcliffe, Custer. (E 1885; I 1897; P 243) County seat. When the rich mines of nearby Silver Cliff began to diminish, a new town was built at the terminus of the Denver & Rio Grande Railroad, about a mile further west. Known first as Clifton, the town was re-named by Dr. W. A. Bell for his birthplace, Westcliff-on-the-Sea, England. Dr. Bell came into the Wet Mountain Valley with Gen. W. J. Palmer in 1870 in search of a southern route for their D&RG Railroad. He was fascinated by the beauty of the area and took up a large tract of land.

Westcreek, Douglas. (E 1895 ?) First a gold camp and supply point for mining camps, prospectors believed the area was a continuation of the Cripple Creek gold belt. The town was named for the district, in turn named for West Creek, a small tributary of Horse Creek, flowing through the town. The official post office name, however, was Pemberton, which honored the first owner of the site. It was a number of years later when the post office name was changed.

Westminster [*West-min'-ster*], Adams. (E 1891; I 1909; P 19,432) The land was once owned by a man named Harris. When the community grew large enough to accommodate a store and post office, it was called Harris Park. In 1891 Stanford White of New York organized a Presbyterian college and named it Westminster and the settlement was incorporated with this name. The college is now the Pillar of Fire Institute.

Weston, Las Animas. (E 1860 ?) Settled in the 1880s by a family headed by Juan Sisneros, a rancher. Though scarcely more than a plaza, it was given the name Los Sisneros. Later in the decade the Rocky Mountain Timber Co. used the settlement as a supply base and several buildings were added to the community. There was no post office until about 1892, when Bert Weston, a blacksmith, was granted the office of postmaster. The town then became known as Weston.

Wetmore, Custer. (E 1880 ?) The site of a stage coach station in pioneer days. William Hayes homesteaded 160 acres in 1880. He sold to Frances Wetmore, whose husband, William, surveyed and named the townsite.

Wheat Ridge, Jefferson. (E 1862 ?; I 1969; P 29,795) Named by State Sen. Henry Lee (1885-89) because this was a thriving wheat growing area. Later orchards and truck farming took the place of wheat fields.

Wheeler Junction, Summit. (E 1880) Now a ghost town, at the junction of West Ten Mile and Ten Mile Creeks. It was settled by homesteader John S. Wheeler and the post office of Wheeler was named for him.

Whitewater, Mesa. (E 1884 ?) The county's fruit industry is said to have originated here when the first orchard was planted in Whitewater. The name comes from Whitewater Creek—because of the high alkali content—and applies to the area as well.

Wiggins, Morgan. (E 1894 ?; I 1974; P 342) For Maj. Oliver P. Wiggins, better known as "Old Scout" Wiggins. A Canadian and once an employee of the Hudson's Bay Co., he came to Colorado about 1834. He was with Fremont on one of the expeditions. The town was called Vallery, then Corona, before it became Wiggins about 1894. (See: Byers and Deer Trail, Colo.)

Wild Horse, Cheyenne. (E 1860 ?) From a nearby creek, once a watering place for immense bands of wild horses. Lieut. Zebulon Pike reported sighting such a band in 1806. When the horses saw Pike's party, they came charging up "making the earth tremble under them like a charge of cavalry."

Wiley, Prowers. (E 1899; I 1909; P 357) The farming center grew when it was reported the Santa Fe Railway would build a line through this area. The settlement was named for W. M. Wiley, one of the town's promoters.

Williamsburg, Fremont. (E 1880; I 1888; P 75) For John Williams, who opened the Williamsburg Mine for the Colorado Fuel & Iron Co.

Willard, Logan. (E 1888). For a Burlington Railroad official.

Windsor [*Win'-zer*], Weld. (E 1882; I 1890; P 1,564) B. H. Eaton, later a state governor (1884-86) established a farm on the present town site, in 1863. In 1880 the post office was called New Liberty, and in January, 1884, postal authorities called it New Windsor, but the town was incorporated as Windsor. The name honors the Rev. A. S. Windsor of Fort Collins, a Methodist circuit minister.

Winter Park, Grand. (E 1923) The town came into existence as a construction camp for the Moffat Tunnel, whose west portal is here. First called West Portal, with the consent of postal authorities the name was changed to Winter Park. This was done with the assistance of Denver Mayor Benjamin F. Stapleton, and many sports enthusiasts, to publicize establishment of the country's top winter sports areas.

Wolcott [*Wohl-kaht'*], Eagle. (E 1889) First known as Bussells, it was the terminus of the Steamboat Springs stage and mail routes, and a supply point for Routt and Grand Counties. The present name honors Colorado U. S. Sen. Edward O. Wolcott (1879-83).

Woodland Park, Teller. (E 1890; I 1891; P 1,022) Before becoming Woodland Park (for the vast stands of pine trees surrounding the settlement) it was known as Summit Park, and Manitou Park.

Woodrow, Washington. (E 1913) Settled by J. A. McGilvray in 1913, the year Woodrow Wilson became president of the United States. The name is said to have been suggested in President Wilson's honor by John Epperson of Brush, Colo.

Woody Creek, Pitkin. (E 1890) The settlement started after discovery of rich gold and silver ores in the vicinity. It probably takes its name from nearby Woody Creek—one of the many generic names in the state.

Wray [*Ray*], Yuma. (E 1886; I 1906; P 1,953) County seat. The town was platted by the See Bar See Land & Cattle Co. and the Lincoln Land Co. Named for John Wray, foreman for I. P. Olive, one of the earliest ranchers in the county.

Yampa [*Yam'-puh*], Routt. (E 1882; I 1907; P 286) A variety of possibilities. Yampa was a division of the Ute Indians who lived in the eastern part of Utah. They were later included under the White River Utes and the name Yampa was not used from then on. Yampa is also the name of a plant whose roots were used by the Indians of Oregon (Carum gairdneri).

Yellow Jacket, Montezuma. (E 1914) When a post office was organized in 1914, the name Yellow Jacket was given, for a nearby canon, the walls of which were plastered with countless yellow jacket nests.

Yoder [*Yoh'-dur*], El Paso. (E 1904) For Ira M. Yoder, a German homesteader, who was active in obtaining a post office for his community. He served as first postmaster.

Yuma [*Yoo'-muh*], Yuma. (E 1886; 1887; P 2,259) Even before farmers started settling the area, there had been a railroad station and water tank on this site. Fred Weld and Ida P. Alrich, through marriage, joined their two quarter sections of land on opposite sides of the railroad and established the townsite. Yuma is the name of an Indian tribe and means "sons of the river."

Boom or "bust" times sometimes ended sadly: with a ghost town.

THOSE COLORFUL COUNTIES

O beautiful for spacious skies,
For amber waves of grain,
For purple mountain majesties
Above the fruited plain!
America! America! God shed His grace on thee,
And crown thy good with brotherhood
From sea to shining sea.

from: "America the Beautiful"
by Katherine Lee Bates.

The State of Colorado is divided by political subdivisions into 63 individual counties—each with an historic name.

This division into counties started with the establishment of the Territory of Colorado in 1861. The Territory's area of 104,246 square miles (approximately 387 miles east-west and 276 miles north-south) was sectioned into 17 organized counties.

Three of these counties—Boulder, Clear Creek, and Gilpin—still retain their original boundaries. In 1909, a subtraction from the southwestern tip of Jefferson was added to Park, after the electors approved this in 1907, followed by a proclamation by the Secretary of State in 1909. These two counties, then, are virtually as originally established in 1861.

Katherine Bates wrote the words above, of her now-national hymn, in 1893, inspired by a trip to Pikes Peak. On a clear day, while you can't "see forever," probably at least a third of Colorado's counties are visible from the apex of the famous peak.

One county name occurs occasionally in the following text but not in the index of counties: Greenwood. It was the only county created and then dissolved—abolished—in Colorado's history.

Greenwood, as well as Bent, was created by the state legislature in 1870 from the eastern parts of El Paso and Pueblo Counties, which reached east to the Kansas border. It was named in honor of William H. Greenwood, chief engineer of the Kansas Pacific Railroad.

Only four years later, general population growth—but lack of it in Greenwood—persuaded the legislature to abolish Greenwood. In 1874

Farm and ranchlands mark the eastern rolling plains.

what was Greenwood was added to part of Douglas to form the new county of Elbert, and the southern part was added to Bent.

The authority for the origin of the names came from LeRoy R. Hafen. In the March, 1931, issue of *The Colorado Magazine*, Dr. Hafen, then state historian, curator, and editor of the magazine, wrote on "The Counties of Colorado." The one and two sentence descriptions of the counties' name origins are Dr. Hafen's. Additional information about the counties came from various authoritative sources, including the now-defunct *Year Book of the State of Colorado*. Figures on the area of the present counties and 1970 populations were supplied by Colorado Counties, Inc., Denver.

Adams. Established 1902. P 185,789. County seat: Brighton. For Gov. Alva Adams, who served two terms and 60 days as governor (1887-89, 97-99, 1905: 66 days). County formed from areas that now include Denver and Arapahoe Counties. Area is 1,237 sq. mi.

Alamosa. [*Al-uh-moh'-suh*]. Established 1913. P 11,422. County seat: Alamosa. For the Spanish word meaning "cottonwood grove." Spanish pioneers gave the name to the creek within the present county. Most recently created of the 63 counties, being formed from Costilla and Conejos Counties. Area is 719 sq. mi.

Arapahoe [*Uh-rap'-uh-hoh*]. Established 1861. P 162,142. County seat: Littleton. For the Arapaho Indians, who long inhabited eastern Colorado. Arapahoe (spelled with an "e") was the first designated Colorado Territory county. Area is 797 sq. mi.

Archuleta [*Ahr-choo-let'-uh*]. Established 1885. P 2,733. County seat: Pagosa Springs. In honor of Antonio D. Archuleta, who was a senator from Conejos County when it was divided to form Archuleta County. Area is 1,364 sq. mi.

Baca [*Bak'-uh*]. Established 1889. P 5,674. County seat: Springfield. For the Baca family of Trinidad, Colo. A member of this family had been the first settler on Two Buttes Creek. The county was created from the eastern portion of Las Animas County. Area is 2,563 sq. mi.

Bent. Established 1874. P 6,493. County seat: Las Animas. From the famous Bent's Fort (located on the north bank of the Arkansas River, midway between La Junta and Las Animas), and from the Bent brothers who founded the fort, 1828-32. Created from a portion of Greenwood County which was established in 1870 and abolished in 1874. Area is 1,519 sq. mi.

Boulder. Established 1861. P 131,889. County seat: Boulder. Named after Boulder City and Boulder Creek, which derived their names from the abundance of boulders in the locality. This is one of original 17 Territorial Counties, and one of three which has its original boundaries. Area is 748 sq. mi.

Chaffee [*Chay'-fee*]. Established 1879. P 10,162. County seat: Salida. In honor of Sen. Jerome B. Chaffee (1825-86), who retired from the United States Senate in the year Chaffee County was created. The county was part of Lake County. Area is 1,038 sq. mi.

Cheyenne [*Shy'-ann*]. Established 1889. P 2,396. County seat: Cheyenne Wells. For the Cheyenne Indians, nomad dwellers of the plains when the settlement of Colorado began. Created from portions of Elbert and Bent Counties. Area is 1,772 sq. mi.

Clear Creek. Established 1861. P 4,819. County seat: Georgetown. So named from the stream that traverses it. The creek was first called Vasquez Fork, but the present name was adopted by 1860. One of the 17 original Territorial Counties, and one of three which have their original boundaries. Area 394 sq. mi.

Conejos [*Kuh-nay'-us*]. Established 1861. P 7,846. County seat: Conejos. The word is Spanish for "rabbits." The name was applied to the principal river of the present county by the Spaniards of New Mexico long before the permanent settlements of the region began. The name was first adopted by the town and then the county. One of the original Territorial Counties. In the county seat Our Lady of Guadalupe, the Catholic Church, oldest church in the state—finished in 1859—is still in use. Area is 1,268 sq. mi.

Costilla [*Kos-tee'-yuh*], Established 1861. P 3,091. County seat: San Luis. Spanish for "rib" and "furring timber." The Costilla River was named by the Spaniards before 1800. The town and county adopted the same name. Another of Colorado Territory's original counties. In the county seat is the oldest store in Colorado, still managed by descendents of the family that established it about 1855. Area is 1,213 sq. mi.

Crowley [*Krow'-lee*]. Established 1911. P 3,086. County seat: Ordway. For John H. Crowley, a State Senator from Otero County at the time that county was divided to form Crowley. Formed from a portion of Otero County. Area is 802 sq. mi.

Custer. Established 1877. P 1,120. County seat: Westcliffe. Named in honor of Gen. George A. Custer, who, with his entire command, was killed by Indians on the Little Bighorn, in present Montana, in June, 1876. Formed from a section of Fremont County. Area is 737 sq. mi.

Delta. Established 1883. P 15,286. County seat: Delta. From the city of Delta, which was so named because of its location on the delta of the

Uncompahgre River. Created from a portion of Gunnison County. Area is 1,154 sq. mi.

Denver. Established 1902. P 514,678. City and county of Denver are identical. In honor of Gen. James W. Denver (1817-1892), governor of Kansas in 1858. When founded, the city of Denver was in Kansas Territory. Denver was the seat of Arapahoe County from its inception in 1861. Denver became a separate entity, from a portion of Arapahoe County, and the only city-county in the state. It has the largest population and the smallest area of the 63 counties. Area is 95 sq. mi.

Dolores [*Duh-loh'-res*]. Established 1881. P 1,641. County seat: Dove Creek. From the Dolores River. The full Spanish name, reported by Father Escalante in 1776, was Rio de Nuestra de los Dolores (River of our Lady of Sorrows). Created from a part of Ouray County. Area is 1,026 sq. mi.

Douglas. Established 1861. P 8,407. County seat: Castle Rock. In honor of Stephen A. Douglas (1813-61), who died in the year of the organization of Colorado's first counties. Area is 843 sq. mi.

Eagle. Established 1883. P 7,498. County seat: Eagle. From the nearby Eagle River. This stream had earlier been called Piney River by General Fremont when he visited it in 1845. Created from a portion of Summit County. Area is 1,682 sq. mi.

Elbert. Established 1874. P 3,903. County seat: Kiowa. In honor of Samuel H. Elbert, Colorado governor when the county was formed. The county—once inhabited by many Indian tribes including the Arapaho, Kiowa, Ute, Cheyenne, and Comanche—was created from a portion of Douglas and the short-lived Greenwood Counties. Area is 1,864 sq. mi.

El Paso [*El Pa'-so*]. Established 1861. P 235,972. County seat: Colorado Springs. The name is Spanish for "the Pass." Ute Pass, west of Colorado Springs, was the famous pass referred to. One of the original 17 Colorado Territory counties and the county in which famous Pikes Peak rises. It is the second most populated county in the state. Area is 2,157 sq. mi.

Fremont [*Free-mahnt'*]. Established 1861. P 21,942. County seat: Canon City. For Gen. John C. Fremont (1813-90), famous western explorer. Another of the original 17 Territorial counties. Near Canon City is the scenic attraction, the Royal Gorge. Area is 1,561 sq. mi.

Garfield. Established 1883. P 14,821. County seat: Glenwood Springs. In honor of President James A. Garfield (1831-81). The county was created from a portion of Summit County. Area is 2,996 sq. mi.

Gilpin [*Gil'pin*]. Established 1861. P 1,272. County seat: Central City. In honor of Col. William Gilpin, first governor of Colorado Territory (1861-62). It is one of the original 17 counties, and one of the three which retains the 1861 boundaries. Next to the City & County of Denver it is the smallest of the 63 counties. Area is 148 sq. mi.

Grand. Established 1874. P 4,107. County seat: Hot Sulphur Springs. Named for Grand Lake and the Grand River. (The river later was renamed the Colorado.) The county was formed from a portion of Summit County. Area is 1,854 sq. mi.

Gunnison. Established 1877. P 7,578. County seat: Gunnison. For Capt. John W. Gunnison, who explored the region in 1853, and who, in the fall of that year, was killed by Indians in Utah. Formed from a portion of Lake County, Gunnison now has the largest body of water—Blue Mesa Reservoir—in the state. Area is 3,220 sq. mi.

Hinsdale [*Hins'-dale*]. Established 1874. P 202. County seat: Lake City. For George A. Hinsdale, prominent pioneer and leader in southern Colorado. He was a former lieutenant governor and died during the month preceding the creation of Hinsdale County. It was formed from portions of Conejos and Summit Counties. Lake City is the only community in the county, which also ranks as the state's least populated. Area is 1,054 sq. mi.

Huerfano [*Wair'-fuh-noh*]. Established 1861. P 6,590. County seat: Walsenburg. The word is Spanish for "orphan." The county was named after the Huerfano River, which in turn from Huerfano Butte, an isolated, cone-shaped butte in the river bottom. Another of the 17 original Territorial counties. Area is 1,574 sq. mi.

Jackson. Established 1909. P 1,811. County seat: Walden. Presumably in honor of President Andrew Jackson. The county was formed from a part of Larimer County. Area is 1,622 sq. mi.

Jefferson. Established 1861. P 233,031. County seat: Golden. From "Jefferson Territory," the extra-legal government that preceded Colorado Territory. The name was adopted in honor of President Thomas Jefferson. It is one of the 17 original Territorial Counties. Its boundaries have changed only slightly from the original lines. It is the third heaviest populated county in the state. Area is 783 sq. mi.

Kiowa [*Kigh'-oh-wah*]. Established 1889. P 2,029. County seat: Eads. For the Kiowa Indians who frequented the region of eastern Colorado in years past. The county was formed from a portion of Bent County. The infamous Sand Creek Massacre took place about eight miles north of the town of Chivington. Area is 1,767 sq. mi.

Kit Carson. Established 1889. P 7,530. County seat: Burlington. In honor of the great western scout, Kit Carson (1809-68). (See under Communities: Kit Carson.) Formed from a part of Elbert County. Area is 2,171 sq. mi.

Lake. Established 1861. P 8,282. County seat: Leadville. Named for the Twin Lakes, outstanding features of the region. One of the original 17 Territorial Counties, although its size has been diminished for creation of other counties. Twin Lakes was once the county seat. Area is 379 sq. miles, third smallest, after Denver and Gilpin Counties.

La Plata [*Luh Plat'-uh*]. Established 1874. P 19,199. County seat: Durango. The name is Spanish for "silver." Silver discoveries in the area by Spaniards during the 18th century fixed the name upon the river and mountains, and it was subsequently given to the county. Formed from portions of Conejos and Lake Counties. Area is 1,683 sq. mi.

Larimer [*Lair'-i-mer*]. Established 1861. P 89,900. County seat: Fort Collins. In honor of Gen William Larimer, a founder of Denver and prominent pioneer of Colorado. Another of the original 17 Territorial counties. More than half of the area of Rocky Mountain National park is within the southwest part of the county. Area is 2,611 sq. mi.

Las Animas. [*Lahs An'-i-muhs*]. Established 1866. P 15,744. County seat: Trinidad. From the principal river of the county. The full name of the stream, discovered and christened by early Spanish explorers, is "El Rio de las Animas Perdidas en Purgatorio" (The River of the Souls Lost in Purgatory). This is the largest of Colorado's 63 counties, formed from Huerfano County, the area being 4,794 sq. mi.

Lincoln. Established 1889. P 4,836. County seat: Hugo. In honor of President Abraham Lincoln. Early, the area was crossed by gold-seekers; later by stockmen, with homesteaders claiming acreage by the late 1890's. Formed from portions of Bent and Elbert Counties. Area is 2,593 sq. mi.

Logan. Established 1887. P 18,852. County seat: Sterling. For Gen. John A. Logan (1826-86), who died shortly before the organization of the county. Created from the eastern portion of Weld County. Area is 1,822 sq. mi.

Mesa [*May'-suh*]. Established 1883. P 54,374. County seat: Grand Junction. The name is a Spanish word for "table." The county took its name from the mesas, or tablelands, common in the region, and perhaps more especially from the Grand Mesa. Formed from part of Gunnison County. Area is 3,301 sq. mi.

Mineral. Established 1893. P 786. County seat: Creede. Its name, and existence, for the many mineral resources of the region. Rich silver ores were discovered in 1890 by Nicholas Creede, for whom the county seat is named. Portions of Mineral, Saguache, and Rio Grande Counties made up the new county. Area is 921 sq. mi.

Moffat [*Mah'-fut*]. Established 1911. P 6,525. County seat: Craig. In honor of David H. Moffat (1839-1911), outstanding Colorado pioneer and railroad builder. The Moffat Road reached Craig in 1913. Moffat's private car, "Marcia," is in use at Craig as the Chamber of Commerce office. The county was created from part of Routt County and is second only to Las Animas County in size. The area is 4,743 sq. mi.

Montezuma [*Mahn-ti-zoo'-muh*]. Established 1889. P 12,952. County seat: Cortez. For the famous chief of the Aztecs of Mexico City, whom Cortez conquered. The prehistoric dewllings in Montezuma County were thought to have been built by the Aztecs. Formed from La Plata County, it is in the southwestern corner of the state. The four corners of Colorado, Arizona, New Mexico, and Utah meet at this point, the only place in the country where this occurs. Area is 2,094 sq. mi.

Montrose [*Mohnt-roz'*]. Established 1883. P 18,366. County seat: Montrose. After the city of Montrose, which is said to have derived its name from Sir Walter Scott's *The Legend of Montrose* (1819). One of the state's natural wonders, Black Canyon of the Gunnison River—2,275 ft. deep—is within the county. It was formed from a portion of Gunnison County. Area is 2,238 sq. mi.

Morgan. Established 1889. P 20,105. County seat: Fort Morgan. From Fort Morgan, the original fort (1865-68), established as protection against the Indians. First called "Junction" or "Camp Wardwell," in 1866 it was named Fort Morgan in honor of Col. Christopher A. Morgan, who died that year. It was created from a part of Weld County. Area is 1,278 sq. mi.

Otero [*Oh-tehr'roh*]. Established 1889. P 23,523. County seat: La Junta. In honor of Miguel Otero, one of the founders of La Junta, and a member of a prominent Spanish family of southern Colorado and New Mexico. Miguel Otero later was appointed Territorial Governor of New Mexico by President McKinley in 1897. The county was formed from Bent County. Area is 1,254. sq. mi.

Ouray [*Oor'-aye*]. Established 1883. P 1,546. County seat: Ouray. For Chief Ouray, distinguished Ute chieftain. (See under Communities: Ouray.) Site of the rich and famous Camp Bird Mine, discovered by Thomas Walsh. His daughter, Evelyn Walsh McLean, was the owner of the celebrated Hope Diamond. The county, formed from San Juan County, is referred to as the "Switzerland of America" because of its spectacular scenery. Area is 540 sq. mi.

Park. Established 1861. P 2,185. County seat: Fairplay. From South Park, which was so named by the early fur traders and trappers. This is one of the four vast park-like areas in the state—the others being North and Middle Parks and the San Luis Valley. Park is one of the original Territorial Counties. Its borders have changed only slightly, once, since it was established. Area is 2,162 sq. mi.

Phillips. Established 1889. P 4,131. County seat: Holyoke. In honor of R. O. Phillips, secretary of the Lincoln Land Co., which organized a number of the towns in eastern Colorado. It was formed from a portion of Logan County. Area is 680 sq. mi.

Pitkin. Established 1881. P 6,185. County seat: Aspen. For Frederick W. Pitkin (1837-86), governor of Colorado when this county was created. The area around Aspen was a rich silver area and the world's largest silver nugget—over a ton in weight—was found in the Smuggler Mine. The county was created from Gunnison County. Area is 973 sq. mi.

Prowers. Established 1889. P 13,258. County seat: Lamar. For John W. Prowers (1838-84), a leading pioneer of the Arkansas Valley. It was Prowers who introduced the first Hereford cattle to the Arkansas Valley, after trailing a herd from Missouri. The county was once part of Bent County. Area is 1,621 sq. mi.

Pueblo [*Pweb'-low*]. Established 1861. P 118,238. County seat: Pueblo. A Spanish word for "town" or "village." The cluster of adobe houses built at the site of the present city of Pueblo in 1841-42 came to be called "the pueblo." The name was adopted by the present city, and then given to the county. (See under Communities: Pueblo.) It is one of the 17 original Territorial counties. Area is 2,405 sq. mi.

Rio Blanco [*Ree'-oh-blahng'-koh*]. Established 1889. P 4,842. County seat: Meeker. Spanish for "White River." The county takes its name from the principal stream of the locality. Escalante, in 1776, named the stream "San Clemente," but the name did not persist. The Rangely oil fields, sixth largest in the United States, are in the west end of the county, which was once part of Garfield County. Area is 3,263 sq. mi.

Rio Grande [*Ree'-oh-grand'*]. Established 1874. P 10,494. County seat: Del Norte. For the large river of the region. The original Spanish name was "Rio Grande del Norte" (Great River of the North). Nearly half of the land area is occupied by the Rio Grande National Forest. The county was created from a portion of Conejos County. Area is 915 sq. mi.

Routt [*Rowt*]. Established 1877. P 6,592. County seat: Steamboat Springs. In honor of John L. Routt (1826-1907), last Territorial and first

State Governor of Colorado. It was at Steamboat Springs Norwegian Karl Howelson demonstrated the art of ski-jumping that led to the area—and other Colorado sections—becoming important in the skiing industry. The county was formed from part of Grand County. Area is 2,330 sq. mi.

Saguache [*Suh-watch'*]. Established 1867. P 3,827. County seat: Saguache. A modified form of the Ute word meaning "blue earth" or "water at the blue earth." The name was applied first to the stream, then to the town, and finally to the county. Saguache was formed from part of Costilla County. Area is 3,144 sq. mi.

San Juan [*San Whan*]. Established 1876. P 831. County seat: Silverton. Spanish for "St. John." The name was given by early Spanish explorers to the river and mountain range, and subsequently was adopted for the general region and this county. Almost three-fourths of the county—which was formed from part of La Plata County—is included in the San Juan National Forest. It is the only county created in the same year Colorado became a state. Area is 391 sq. mi.

San Miguel [*San Mih-gil'*]. Established 1883. P 1,194. County seat: Telluride. Spanish for "St. Michael." The name was first given to the river and later to the county. San Miguel was formed from a portion of Ouray County. Area is 1,283 sq. mi.

Sedgwick. Established 1889. P 3,405. County seat: Julesburg. For Fort Sedgwick (1864-71). The military post, across the river from present Ovid, was named in honor of Gen. John Sedgwick, killed in the Civil War in 1864. He had led Indian campaigns into the region of Colorado in 1857 and 1860. The county was created in the extreme northeast corner of the state from part of Logan County. Area is 544 sq. mi.

Summit. Established 1861. P 2,665. County seat: Breckenridge. For the mountainous character of the territory. The eastern boundary of the original county followed "the summit of the snowy range" from a point a little south of Breckenridge to the Wyoming line. One of the original 17 Territorial counties and embracing a vast area. Portions were used to create other counties and its area now is 604 sq. mi.

Teller. Established 1899. P 3,316. County seat: Cripple Creek. In honor of the U.S. Senator Henry M. Teller (1830-1914). Teller, called the "Silver Senator" because of his role in advocating "free silver," served from 1876-82 and 1885-1909. The county, one of the many great precious-metal producing in the state, was formed from portions of El Paso and Fremont Counties. Area is 553 sq. mi.

Washington. Established 1887. P 5,550. County seat: Akron. For President George Washington. Texas longhorn cattle were grazed in the region in the 1870's, and cattle raising still is important to the economy. It also is a wheat center and the county has a large petroleum production. The county was once part of Weld County. Thirty-one states have counties named for the first U.S. president. Area is 2,526 sq. mi.

Weld. Established 1861. P 89, 297. County seat: Greeley. In honor of Lewis Ledyard Weld, first Secretary of Colorado Territory. It is one of the richest agricultural counties in the nation, ranking among the leaders in cattle, sugar beets, barley, beans, onions, corn, tomatoes, and cucumbers as well as oil. It was one of the 17 original Territorial counties. While its size has diminished from the forming of other counties, it ranks third in total area, which is 4,002 sq. mi.

Yuma [*Yoo'-muh*]. Established 1889. P 8,544. County seat: Wray. For the Yuma Indians, who lived near the mouth of the Colorado River. It is an agricultural area, comprised almost entirely of farms and ranches, and there is great emphasis on fine cattle herds. The county was formed from part of Washington. Today the area is 2,379 sq. mi.

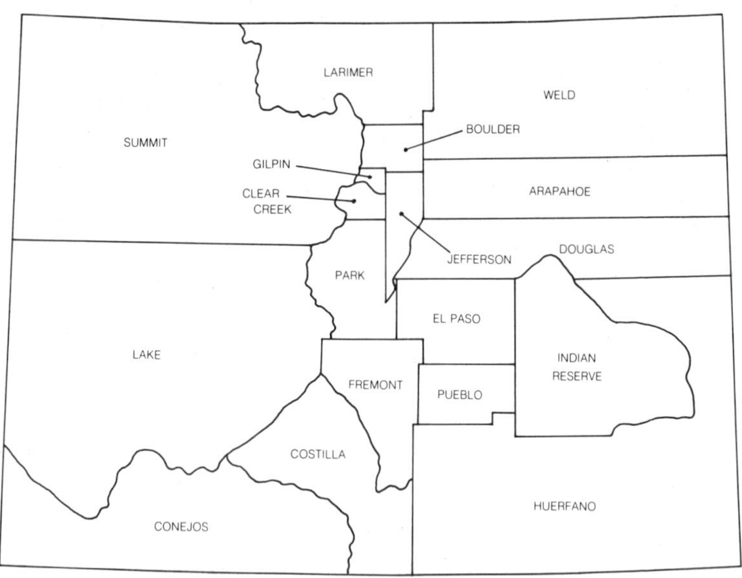

Colorado Territory, established in 1861, started with 17 counties.

The wide-open West still remains in the vast counties.

THE ELITE PEAKS

I'm looking at your lofty head
  Away up in the air
Eight thousand feet above the plain
  Where grows the prickly-pear.
A great big thing with ice on
  You seem to be up there.

Away above the timber-line
  You lift your frosty head,
Where lightnings are engendered,
  And thunderstorms are bred;
But you'd be a bigger tract of land
  If you were thin out-spread.

from: "New Colorado and the Santa
Fe Trail." (1880)
—Anon.

The mile-high state has, it may be seen from the last two lines above, long endured the comments it would be "bigger than Texas" if the soaring mountains could be leveled. In that case there wouldn't be this section on the 14,000 ft. peaks.

There are 53 peaks and mountains in Colorado rising to 14,000 ft. or more, above sea-level—a greater number than any of the other contiguous states. As for the lesser mountains—10,000 to 13,000 footers—the number is almost incalcuable. However, these provide the setting for the rugged natural sky-scrapers that are so showy. (A *Colorado Year Book* figure of several years ago stated 1,143 mountains had an elevation of 10,000 feet or more above sea level with 53 over 14,000 and 831 from 11,000 to 14,000 feet.)

Interestingly, the heights of these natural sky-scrapers have varied through the years. More accurately, the heights have remained constant but the official measurements have been altered. For example, Pikes Peak is ranked 31st highest in the state as new measurements have raised (and sometimes lowered) other ranking peaks. Back in 1931 Pikes was ranked 28th.

Colorado's mightiest: Mt. Elbert. Half-Moon Creek in foreground.

Mention is made in the following section of name origins to various survey parties or personnel. The major organized surveys started in 1869. The names of the parties have included: Harvard, Princeton, Hayden, Wheeler, Land Office, United States Geological Survey, Colorado Geological Survey, and United States Coast and Geodetic Survey. Today the USGS provides periodic changes (if any).

Much of the name-origin data has come from *Fourteen Thousand Feet*, by John L. Jerome Hart, a 1972 reprint of the 1931 second edition of the book published by the Colorado Mountain Club. Some information has come from the State Historical Society of Colorado, and some from *The Fourteeners*, by Perry Eberhart and Philip Schmuck. Hart's book provides some details of early ascents while the latter volume is basically a beautiful photo-essay.

Peaks and mountains are listed in descending order of their heights, with the latest elevations as provided by the USGS.

Mt. Elbert. Lake. 14,433 ft. For Samuel Elbert, appointed by President Lincoln as secretary of Colorado Territory, under Territorial Gov. John Evans. In 1873 President Grant appointed Elbert sixth governor of Colorado Territory. He served until 1874, when he resigned. He was elected to the state Supreme Court and served from 1877-82 and 1886-88. Elbert married a daughter of John Evans. The mountain is Colorado's highest. It was named prior to Elbert's term as governor. A Colorado county also bears his name.

Mt. Massive. Lake. 14,421 ft. Just 12 feet shorter than neighbor and number one peak, Elbert, the mountain was apparently named early by miners for its massive size. It is broad, bulky, and spectacular. Henry Gannett, topographer with the Hayden Surveys, was probably the first man to climb the peak.

Mt. Harvard. Chaffee. 14,420 ft. Colorado's third-ranking peak, and highest in the Collegiate Group in the Sawatch Range. Named and measured in 1869 by Prof. J. D. Whitney, first head of the Harvard Mining School. Many of the members of Whitney's survey party included first graduates of the Harvard school.

Blanca Peak [*Blang'-kuh*]. Alamosa, Costilla, Huerfano. 14,345 ft. A Spanish word for "white," as its crest is nearly always crowned with snow. The name Sierra (Mountain) Blanca covers a group of mountains including Blanca, Baldy, Little Bear, Middle Creek, and Twin Peaks. Blanca Peak is the highest of the group.

La Plata Peak [*La Plat'-uh*]. Chaffee. 14,336 ft. Named for the La Plata mining district in 1874 by F. V. Hayden. The word is Spanish, meaning "silver." Much early mining activity—at least evidence of prospectors—has been noted above timberline. A much-quoted saying goes: "A good silver-mine / Is above timberline / Ten times out of nine."

Uncompahgre Peak [*Un-cum-pah'-gray*]. Hinsdale. 14,309 ft. For the Uncompahgre River, named by the Ute Indians. Literally translated it means hot (unca) water (pah) spring (gre) (pronounced: un-cum-pa-gray). The name is traced back to the early 1850's.

Crestone Peak. Custer, Saguache. 14,294 ft. For its resemblance to a "cock's comb," in the Spanish vernacular. Other interpretations of the word, however, include: crest, crests, outcropping of ore, helmet crest. It has two neighbors—Kit Carson Peak and Crestone Needle—which, with their jagged outlines, make up the appearance of a cock's comb.

Lincoln Peak. Park. 14,286 ft. For President Abraham Lincoln. Wilbur F. Stone, then a placer miner and later a famed jurist and Colorado historian, climbed the peak in 1861. Impressed by the mountain and the view from the summit, he asked fellow citizens to select a name appropriate for a magnificent mountain. The present name was the concensus. In 1864 area miners sent the president a gold retort valued at $800.

Grays Peak. Clear Creek, Summit. 14,270 ft. For a celebrated botanist, Asa Gray, and named in 1861 by Charles C. Parry, who also named nearby Torreys Peak. Earlier the pair was known to prospectors as the "Twin Peaks" and as "Ant Hills" to the Indians.

Mt. Antero. Chaffee. 14,269 ft. For a Ute Indian Chief, Antero, who, with others of his tribe, signed a treaty between the Utes and the United States in 1878.

Torreys Peak. Clear Creek, Summit. 14,267 ft. For John Torrey, botanist as reknowned as Asa Gray, and named (with Grays Peak) by C. C. Parry. There had been talk that it should be named for Richard Irwin, an early miner. In 1872 a party, including peaks-namer Parry, climbed Grays Peak, and the two peaks' names became official from that time. Torrey and Gray named many of the region's flora. They collaborated in 1831 on the first part of the *Flora of North America*, and have been called America's first botanists.

Castle Peak. Gunnison, Pitkin. 14,265 ft. Named by the Hayden Survey because its noticable "towers" along the ridges resembled the outline of a European castle. Purple in color, it is the highest of the Elk Range.

Mt. Evans. Clear Creek. 14,264 ft. First named Rosalie by Albert Bierstadt, the painter, in 1863, but renamed Evans in 1870, honoring the second Territorial governor (1862-65). Evans' name is also on a town, and a Denver avenue—which fronts Denver University of which he was a founder. The D.U. Cosmic Ray Research Laboratory was built on the summit in 1936, reached by what is probably the highest road in the world. The name Rosalie (for Bierstadt's wife) was given to a nearby mountain. Mount Evans is supposed to be the "model" for one of Bierstadt's famous paintings, "Storm in the Rocky Mountains."

Quandary Peak. Summit. 14,264 ft. The dictionary term is: a state of perplexity or doubt. So were prospectors in the early 1860's at strange outcroppings of silver ore in the area. The mountain to be known as Quandary had a claim staked—the Quandary Lode—and the name came to be permanent in 1869.

Longs Peak. Boulder. 14,256 ft. For Maj. Stephen D. Long, whose exploring expedition (1819-20) came into what was to be Colorado. Earlier known as The Two Ears (a French translation) and The Two Guides (Arapaho Indian translation)—coupling Longs with Mount Meeker (13,911 ft.) to the south. Longs name was applied about 1825. It was never spelled with an apostrophe, per ruling of the U.S. Board of Geographic Names.

Mt. Wilson. Dolores. 14,246 ft. Named for A. D. Wilson, chief topographer for the Hayden Survey in 1874, and who climbed the peak in that year. Although another name—Glacier—was applied by the Wheeler Survey, it was ruled the Wilson name would remain. Wilson, a true mountaineer, also climbed Mt. Rainier, in Washington, in 1870, only two months after its first ascent. Oddly, nearby Wilson Peak (ranked 47th in Colorado) also is named for this topographer-climber.

Mt. Shavano [*Shav'-uh-noh*]. Chaffee. 14,229 ft. For Ute Indian Chief Shavano, a signer of a convention between the Utes and the United States in 1873. Spelled "Chavanaux"—and signed with an X, his was the fourth of 133 signers—one of four chiefs. He remained loyal to the U.S. in an 1879 uprising. His name appears on maps showing the peak after that date. Deep crevices on the east side of Mt. Shavano, in spring and early summer, fill with snow and create a figure known as the "Angel of Shavano." The standing figure—arms outstretched—is the subject of numerous Indian legends.

Mt. Princeton. Chaffee. 14,197 ft. Another in the Collegiate Group, named for Princeton College. First known as Chalk Mountain, from Chalk Creek at its base, the present name was probably given by Henry Gannet. The name has been in use since at least 1873.

Mt. Belford. Chaffee. 14,197 ft. Supposedly named for Colorado Territorial Judge James Belford, appointed by President U.S. Grant in 1870. He retired from the bench in 1875, and when Colorado became a state in 1876, was elected as the first representative to the U.S. House of

Representatives. In Washington he was nicknamed the "Red-Headed Rooster of the Rockies," because of colorful manner and appearance. The peak was a latecomer to the roster of the 14,000 ft. ranks as it was considered part of Mt. Oxford. Later surveys added height, and designation as a separate peak.

Mt. Yale. Chaffee. 14,196 ft. Third in the Collegiate Group, and named by Prof. J. D. Whitney, head of the Harvard Mining School and head of an 1869 survey, for Yale University. Whitney was a graduate of Yale in 1839.

Crestone Needle. Custer. 14,191 ft. Part of the Crestone Group—Crestone Peak, Kit Carson Peak, Humboldt Peak. The spire of Crestone Needle is capped by a thimble-like summit. The name means, broadly, a cock's comb. (See: Crestone Peak.)

Mt. Bross [*Br-ohs'*]. Park. 14,172 ft. For William Bross, Lieutenant-Governor of Illinois (1813-89), who owned mining property near Alma, Colo. Writer Samuel Bowles and Bross together climbed Grays peak and probably Mt. Lincoln in 1868. Father John Dyer in his book, *The Snow Shoe Itinerant*, states Bross was so enthused at the Lincoln climb "the boys called peak of Lincoln, Mt. Bross."

Kit Carson Peak. Saguache. 14,165 ft. Named by F. V. Hayden for the frontier scout, Kit Carson, well known in the area. At one time Carson was commander of Fort Massachusetts, at the foot of Blanca Peak. Earlier names include "Haystack Baldy" and "Frustum."

El Diente Peak. [*El Dee-ehn'-tee*]. Dolores. 14,159 ft. Spanish for "the tooth," for its jagged outline resembling a tooth. A steep mountain, El Diente is said to be one of Colorado's most demanding peaks to climb.

Maroon Peak. Pitkin. 14,156 ft. Locally known as Maroon Bells (North Maroon Peak and South Maroon Peak), named for its coloration by the Hayden Survey. Originally called Maroon Mountain, because a peak cannot ordinarily have two peaks while a mountain can have two or more peaks. The Maroon Bells are so distinctive they are often shown as calendar art.

Mt. Tabeguache. [*Mt. Tay-bih-wash'*]. Chaffee. 14,155 ft. For a tribe of Ute Indians of which Shavano (see Mt. Shavano) was chief. It was a known but unnamed mountain for many years, and until rather recently, was not known to be over 14,000 ft. in height. The name was given by the Colorado Mountain Club.

Mt. Oxford. Chaffee. 14,153 ft. Another in the Collegiate Group, but neglected until about 1925 when it was named—in keeping with the other college names—by the Colorado Mountain Club.

Mt. Sneffles. Ouray. 14,150 ft. Supposedly after a passage in Jules Verne's *Journey to the Center of the Earth* mentioning Mount Sneffels (or Snaaefell). The name dates back to at least 1890.

Mt. Democrat. Lake, Park. 14,148 ft. Originally known as Buckskin on Hayden's map for a town near its base named for Joseph (Buckskin Joe) Higginbottom. Supposedly some Southerners had called the peak for their political party—and the name remained. It became Mt. Democrat on maps after the Land Office Survey in 1883.

Capitol Peak. Pitkin. 14,130 ft. For its stately form, and named by the Hayden Survey. Earlier called "The Twins" for Capitol and Snowmass Peaks; another naming for the two was Capitol and Whitehouse—obviously for the two buildings in the District of Columbia. Only the Capitol name was retained.

Pikes Peak. El Paso. 14,110 ft. Probably one of America's best known mountains, named for its known discoverer, Lt. Zebulon Pike. Though Pike saw it during his expedition of 1806, he called it "Grand Peak." In 1820, during the Long Expedition, it was called James Peak for Edwin James, Long's botanist. Apparently the final namer was Col. Henry Dodge who used the name Pikes Peak on his map of 1835. The name gained prominence during the early Colorado gold rush—the area being known as Pikes Peak country. It was first climbed by James. An auto road and a cog railroad go to the summit of the famous mountain.

Snowmass Peak. Gunnison, Pitkin. 14,092 ft. Named by F. V. Hayden for the mass of snow which gathered on the eastern side of the peak. It was a latecomer to the ranks of the 14,000 ft. elite. Along with Capitol Peak, it was one of the once-known "Twins," and was the "White House" peak when Capitol and now-Snowmass were so designated in earlier years. (See Capitol Peak.)

Windom Peak. La Plata. 14,087 ft. For William Windom (1827-91), who was a U.S. Representative and Senator (though not from Colorado), and Secretary of the Treasury under President Garfield. No special significance was attached to the naming. The United States Geological Survey representative mapping the area was to name 30 summits; Windom was among the last named, as was nearby Sunlight Peak—also a name without significance.

Mt. Eolus [*Mt. Ee'-oh-lus*]. La Plata. 14,084 ft. First mentioned in the Hayden Survey of 1874 as Mount Aeolus—the Greek God of the Winds. The present spelling, Eolus, was used by the Wheeler Survey in 1878.

Mt. Columbia. Chaffee. 14,073 ft. Still another in the Collegiate Group, and one of the last named for a school. Denverite Roger W. Toll named it about 1916 and the name was adopted by the Colorado Mountain Club in 1922.

Culebra Peak [*Koo-lay'-brah*]. Costilla. 14,069 ft. While the word in Spanish means "snakes," it is thought it refers to the winding river—the Culebra—rather than snakes on the peak. It is an early name, appearing on Lieutenant Pike's map of 1810 (Rio de la Culebra), and others which followed.

Missouri Mountain. Chaffee. 14,067 ft. Because it was connected by ridges to neighbors Mt. Oxford and Mt. Harvard, Missouri was not known as a separate mountain. However, in 1956 the U.S. Geological Survey gave it a separate identity and elevation. The name stems from the state. It's possible the namer injected a bit of humor on the separation of Missouri from Oxford, thinking of the "show me" nickname of Missouri.

Humboldt Peak. Custer. 14,064 ft. Part of the Crestone Group in the Sangre de Cristo Range, this peak takes its name from Alexander van Humboldt. He was a German and famous in the 19th century as a explorer, mountaineer, traveller, and geographer. A German colony was started in the Wet Mountain Valley, and one of the best-producing mines the colonists discovered was named the Humboldt.

Mt. Bierstadt. [*Mt. Beer'-stahd*]. Clear Creek. 14,060 ft. For Albert Bierstadt, a painter whose works became world-famous, with three being painted for the Capitol in Washington, D.C. One of his most popular is "Storm over the Rockies," with Mt. Evans as the model. When the Front Range was still known as the Chicago Mountains, Bierstadt named what is now Evans, Rosalie, for his wife.

Sunlight Peak. La Plata. 14,059 ft. Named by the U.S. Geological Survey in 1902, but without special meaning; possibly the peak was flooded with sunshine when it was named! (See Windom Peak.)

Handies Peak. Hinsdale. 14,048 ft. Supposedly for a San Juan area man of some repute, perhaps a surveyor. Whatever his credentials, his surname apparently was given to the peak rather early. The Hayden Survey noted in 1874 the name Handies was already in use.

Mt. Lindsey. Costilla. 14,042 ft. Until 1954 the name was "Old Baldy," applied in the 1870's. The name now honors Malcolm Lindsey, Trinidad, Colo., born, a climber of the peak in his youth, and a prominent Denver attorney for much of his life. He was active in the Colorado Mountain Club, which sponsored the change in name.

Little Bear Peak. Costilla. 14,037. Now the only animal name for a 14,000 ft. Colorado peak (another once was Grizzley Mountain, since resurveyed at slightly less than 14,000 ft.). The name comes from Little Bear Creek at its foot. An earlier name was West Peak. It was first scaled about 1888.

Mt. Sherman. Lake, Park. 14,036 ft. Apparently for Civil War General William T. Sherman, but without any other historical significance. It first appeared on a map of the area in 1881.

Redcloud Peak. Hinsdale. 14,034 ft. Named for its ruddy coloration and because the upper ridges are said to resemble clouds. First called Red Mountain, it was named Red Cloud by Hayden's Survey in 1874. The name now is spelled as one word.

Pyramid Peak. Pitkin. 14,018 ft. Named by the Hayden Survey for its pyramidal outline and early called Black Pyramid as well as Pyramid. G. M. Wheeler, in his survey about the same time, termed Pyramid one of the state's "most spectacular" mountains.

Wilson Peak. San Miguel. 14,017 ft. For A. D. Wilson, chief topographer for the Hayden Survey. It is next to Mount Wilson, also named for the mountaineer. (See Mt. Wilson.)

Wetterhorn Peak. Hinsdale, Ouray. 14,017 ft. Thought to have been named for the well-known Swiss alp, which it somewhat resembles, by the Wheeler Survey in 1874. Strangely, little seems to be known about the name—it appears on Wheeler maps but not on Hayden Survey maps—thus leading to the above conclusion.

North Maroon Peak. Pitkin. 14,014 ft. One of the twin Maroon Bells, and thought by the Hayden Survey to be one: Maroon Mountain. Distinctive for its shape and color. (See Maroon Peak.)

San Luis Peak. Saguache. 14,014 ft. Thought to be transferred from the San Luis Valley at its foot. Spanish for Saint Louis, the town of San Luis, named for its parton saint, is the oldest community in Colorado.

Huron Peak. Chaffee. 14,005 ft. A latecomer to the high peaks, Huron, probably named for the Indian tribe, was resurveyed and topped the 14,000 ft. mark in 1956.

Mount of the Holy Cross. Eagle. 14,005 ft. Named for the huge cross of snow—1,400 ft. tall, about 450 ft. wide—in crevices on its east face. First photographed by William H. Jackson in 1873, and painted by artist Thomas Moran later, it became almost as famous as Pikes Peak. Crumbling rocks have caused the cross to lose some of its outline. President Hoover proclaimed the area around the peak a National Monument in 1929. It was only in recent years that resurveying showed its elevation as slightly over 14,000 ft.

Sunshine Peak. Hinsdale. 14,001 ft. Named by the U.S. Geological Survey about 1904, although no explanation was given for the choice. Again (as in the case of Sunlight Peak), perhaps it was viewed in bright sunshine. The Hayden Survey apparently camped on the peak, calling it simply "Station 12." Before its official naming, it was known as Niagra and to some as Sherman. Earlier it was considered several feet higher, but recent surveys still show it to be of the elite 14,000 ft. class.

Portrait by nature: Snow-covered Echo Lake and majestic Mt. Evans.

MAJOR MOUNTAIN PASSES

If you want to know where it was,
I stopped my car
On the hump of Hardscrabble Pass up Hardscrabble Creek
To stare across the blue Wet Mountain Valley
And listen to the far-off sawtooth snag
Of the Sangré de Cristo Mountains ripping slabs
Of purple from the sky and letting them fall
All purple over purple long ago.

from: "Report of My Strange Encounter
With Lilly Bull-Domingo"
by Thomas Hornsby Ferril.

A mountain pass is a low place in a mountain range. Sometimes the designation is "divide," sometimes "saddle," or "gap," A pass provides an easy—or perhaps easier—crossing for trails and roads.

The Colorado State Highway Department has noted almost 300 passes of which five have the name "saddle," six "divide," and 12 "gap."

Only 34 of these are on highways indexed on the official highway map. The origin of the names, the county or counties in which they lie, and their elevations are mentioned—plus a bit of history—in the folllowing listing.

Not included in the 34 is Hardscrabble Pass mentioned in the Ferril poem. It still exists, as it has since the 1870's, near Westcliffe; altitude 8,800 ft. A state gazetteer now calls it Hardscrabble Saddle. The name was taken from Hardscrabble Creek. About 1845 a number of Ute Indians are supposed to have surprised and killed some settlers along the Huerfano River. Those who escaped followed up an unnamed stream. They described their flight as a "hard scrabble" or "hard scramble," and the creek was thus known from that time.

That name is not uncommon, being used at various times on various frontiers, always meaning meagre results at great effort.

Chief source for the reasons for the names of the passes was the library of the State Historical Society of Colorado, with assists from *The Great Gates*, a story of the Rocky Mountain Passes, by Coloradan Marshall Sprague. This book recounts and lists passes in all the Rocky Mountain

Trail Ridge Road, highest continuous highway in the U.S.

states and is good reading. For those wishing to explore most of the Colorado passes there is *Mountain Passes* by Clyde and Chloe Edmondsom, a detailed "how to" guide for hikers and drivers; no name nomenclature, however.

The listing of the major highway passes is in alphabetical order.

Berthoud Pass [*Berth'-ud*]. 11,314 ft. For Capt. Edward L. Berthoud, discoverer, in 1861, of the pass which now bears his name. He was also chief engineer of the Colorado Central Railroad. (See: Berthoud, Colo.) On Continental Divide, Clear Creek and Grand Counties.

Cucharas Pass [*Coo-chair'-us*]. 9,994 ft. A Spanish word meaning "spoon" or "spoon-shaped." In the Sangre de Cristo Range. (See: Cuchara, Colo.) In Huerfano and Las Animas Counties.

Cumbres Pass [*Kuhm'-burs*]. 10,022 ft. Another Spanish word, this meaning "crests." Visible from the pass is the scenic Cumbres & Toltec Railroad (formerly the narrow-gauge Denver & Rio Grande Railroad) which dates back to 1880. In Conejos County.

Dallas Divide. 8,970 ft. For U.S. Vice President George M. Dallas (1845-49). It follows the route laid out by road-builder, railroad-builder Otto Mears in the 1880's. In Ouray and San Miguel Counties.

Douglas Pass. 8,268 ft. For a White River Ute Indian chief, Douglas. It was Douglas's warriors who killed Nathan Meeker in 1879. Spanish explorer, Father Escalante, is said to have crossed this pass in 1776. (See: Meeker, Colo.) In Garfield County.

Fremont Pass. 11,318 ft. For Explorer John C. Fremont, who is not known to have crossed it—but did travel over other nearby passes. (See: Fremont County.) On Continental Divide, Lake and Summit Counties.

Gore Pass. 9,524 ft. For English sportsman, Sir Charles Gore. The fabulous, extrovert hunter spent considerable time in the area and his deeds are near legend. In Grand County.

Hoosier Pass. 11,541 ft. Supposedly named about 1860 by gold-hunting prospectors from Indiana, the "Hoosier State." On Continental Divide, Park and Summit Counties. (Another Hoosier Pass is in Teller County.)

Independence Pass. 12,095 ft. For the town of Independence near the crest (and now a ghost town), which was founded on Independence Day, 1879. On Continental Divide, Lake and Pitkin Counties.

Kenosha Pass. 10,001 ft. For Kenosha, Wis., by a stage coach driver whose home had been there. The word in the Chippewa Indian language is supposed to mean a pike (fish). In Park County.

La Manga Pass. 10,230 ft. A Spanish term, translated as "The Sleeve." In Conejos County.

Lizard Head Pass. 10,222 ft. For nearby Lizard Head Peak (13,156 ft.), which derives its name from its peculiar, lizard-head-like shape. In Dolores and San Miguel Counties.

Loveland Pass. 11,992 ft. For W.A.H. Loveland, president of the Colorado Central Railroad. The highway, U.S. 6, while still in use, has been succeeded by the Eisenhower Tunnel, on Interstate 70, boring through the Continental Divide. (See: Loveland, Colo.) On Continental Divide, Clear Creek and Summit Counties.

McClure Pass. 8,755 ft. For Thomas McClure, who is famous as a developer of the Red McClure potato. In Gunnison and Pitkin Counties.

Milner Pass. 10,759 ft. For T.J. Milner, an accomplished early-day civil engineer for both railroads and street car lines. On Continental Divide, Grand and Larimer Counties.

Molas Divide [*Mole'-us*]. 10,910 ft. For the moles in moist ground of adjacent Molas Lake, according to one source. Another authority asserts there are no moles in Colorado. Undoubtedly the pass was named after nearby Molas Lake. The word does not appear in contemporary atlases, for any city or place. In San Juan County.

Monarch Pass. 11,312 ft. For an early (1880's) mining camp called Monarch. The townsite was near the present limestone quarry operations on the east side of the pass. On Continental Divide, Chaffee and Gunnison Counties.

Muddy Pass. 8,772 ft. For Big Muddy Creek, a tributary of the Colorado River. Probably named when its waters were roiled by storm. On Continental Divide, Grand and Jackson Counties. (Not to be confused with Muddy Creek Pass.)

North La Veta Pass [*La Veet'-uh*]. 9,413 ft. Spanish for "The Vein," probably referring to the mineral veins from West Spanish Peak. (See: La Veta, Colo.) In Costilla and Huerfano Counties.

North Cochetopa Pass [*Kohch-i-toh'-puh*]. 10,149 ft. A Ute Indian word meaning "pass of the buffalo." The original pass, to the south, was once an Indian and buffalo trail between what is now the vast San Luis

Valley and the Gunnison area. On Continental Divide, Saguache County.

Poncha Pass. 9,010 ft. Possibly for the Spanish word for "paunch" or "belly," describing the low gap in the mountains; possibly meaning "mild." One source indicates Poncha is a derivation of Ponca, one of the five tribes of the Siouan Indian family. In Gunnison and Saguache Counties.

Rabbit Ears Pass. 9,426 ft. For the formation of nearby Rabbit Ears Peak, somewhat resembling rabbit ears. On Continental Divide, Grand and Jackson Counties.

Red Hill Pass. 9,993 ft. Probably for a reddish colored mountain. Red Hill was mentioned in *The Snow Shoe Itinerant,* by the Rev. John Dyer, in the 1860's. In Park County. (Not to be confused with other "Red" passes.)

Red Mountain Pass. 11,018 ft. For the mountain itself, as is Red Mountain Creek. Once the location of Otto Mears's narrow-gauge Silverton Railroad. In Ouray and San Juan Counties. (Another Red Mountain Pass is not on a highway.)

Slumgullion Pass. 11,361 ft. Named for the varicolored rocks of a vast, ancient slide, resembling the colors of a slumgullion (stew). In Hinsdale County.

Squaw Pass. 9,807 ft. Formerly known as Soda Hill Pass, the present name was adopted by the Colorado Geographic Board in 1916. It is presumed an Indian-type name was desired, though the board minutes give no details. In Clear Creek County. (Another Squaw Pass is in western Colorado.)

Tennessee Pass. 10,424 ft. For the southern state, supposedly by goldminers from Tennessee, in the 1860's. On Continental Divide, Eagle and Lake Counties.

Trail Ridge High Point. 12,183 ft. For its route in traversing part of an old Indian ridge trail. The highest continuous highway in the United States. In Larimer County.

Trout Creek Pass. 9,346 ft. For the stream, Trout Creek. This is a very old Indian trail, and used by early Colorado railroads in the 1880's. In Chaffee and Park Counties.

Ute Pass. 6,800 ft. For an old Ute trail which passes the north side of Pikes Peak. The one-time Colorado Midland Railroad followed the same route. In El Paso County. (There are four other passes named Ute.)

Vail Pass. 10,603 ft. For Colorado Highway Dept. Chief Engineer, Charles D. Vail. It was little used until the highway was constructed in 1940. (See: Vail, Colo.) In Eagle and Summit Counties.

Wilkerson Pass. 9,507 ft. Probably for an early-day rancher of the region. However, no details about the name are recorded. In Park County.

Willow Creek Pass. 9,683 ft. For the stream, Willow Creek (undoubtedly for its willow bushes), and used as an Indian trail. It became a road in the early 1900's. On Continental Divide, Grand and Jackson Counties.

Wolf Creek Pass. 10,850 ft. For the stream on the west side, probably for early day timber wolves in the area. On Continental Divide, Mineral County.

The Collegiate Range dwarfs west approach to Trout Creek Pass.

BIBLIOGRAPHY

Following are the major works used in researching *Colorado Place Names:*

Arps, Louisa Ward, and Elinor Eppich Kingery. *High Country Names.* Estes Park, Colo.: Rocky Mountain Nature Assn., 1972 (Revised edition).

Baskette, Floyd. *Pronunciation Guide: Colorado.* np, nd (Boulder, 1952).

Bauer, William H., James L. Ozment, and John H. Willard. *Colorado Postal History.* Crete, Neb.: J-B Publishing Co., 1971.

Colorado Magazine. Denver: State Historical Society of Colorado, Vol. VIII, No. 2 (March, 1931).

Colorado Magazine. Denver: State Historical Society of Colorado, Vol. XVII, No. 1 to Vol. XX, No. 3 (January, 1940-May, 1943).

Colorado Year Book, 1959-61. Denver: State Planning Commission, nd.

Davidson, Levette J., and Olga H. Koehler. "The Naming of Colorado's Towns and Cities," in *American Speech,* February, 1932.

Eberhart, Perry, and Philip Schmuck. *The Fourteeners.* Chicago: The Swallow Press, 1970.

Fay, Albert H. *A Glossary of the Mining and Mineral Industry.* Washington: Government Printing Office, 1920.

Gannet, Henry. *A Gazetteer of Colorado.* Washington: Government Printing Office, 1906.

Gannett, Henry. *Origin of Certain Place Names in the United States.* Washington: Government Printing Office, 1902 (Reprinted 1971).

Griswold, Don, and Jean Griswold. *Colorado's Century of Cities.* np, nd (Denver, 1958).

Hart, John L. Jerome. *Fourteen Thousand Feet.* Denver: Colorado Mountain Club, 1931 (Reprinted 1972).

Matthews, Ruth E. "A Study of Colorado's Place Names." (Master's thesis, Stanford, Calif., 1940).

Pearl, Richard M. *Nature's Names for Colorado's Communities.* Colorado Springs: Earth Science Publishing Co., 1975.

Sprague, Marshall. *The Great Gates.* Boston: Little Brown & Co., 1964.

United States Census of Population, 1970. Washington: Government Printing Office.

Stewart, George R. *American Place-Names.* New York: Oxford University Press, 1970.

Stewart, George R. *Names on the Land.* Boston: Houghton Mifflin Co., 1958 (revised edition).

Wilkins, Tivis E. *Colorado Railroads.* Boulder: Pruett Press, 1974.

The tank is lonesome, sun-bleaching. No train today. Not ever.

ACKNOWLEDGEMENTS

While most of the research for *Colorado Place Names* was done in Denver, at the State Historical Society of Colorado Library and the Western History Department of the Denver Public Library, many other libraries, organizations, and individuals made valuable contributions. For their responses with helpful information, a heartfelt thanks.

The public libraries include: Aspen (Pitkin County), Canon City, Colorado Springs (Pikes Peak Regional), Cortez, Delta, Eagle (Eagle County), Fort Collins, Frisco (Summit County), Golden, Kiowa (Elbert County), La Junta (Woodruff Memorial), Lakewood, Longmont, Pueblo (Pueblo Regional District), Stratton, Walden (Jackson County), and Wray (Northeast Colorado Regional).

Other libraries: Adams State College, Alamosa, and Fort Lewis College, Durango.

Other institutions: Park County Historical Society, Bailey; Rio Grande County Museum, Del Norte; Municipal Museum, Greeley; Lincoln County Historical Society, Hugo; Rio Blanco County Historical Society, Meeker; Routt County Historical Society, Steamboat Springs; and Chambers of Commerce at Buena Vista, Craig, and Fort Morgan.

Also: Petroleum Information, Inc., Colorado Counties, Inc., and the Colorado State Highway Department, Denver; State Historical Society of Wisconsin, Madison; Atchison, Topeka and Santa Fe Railway Co., Topeka, and Missouri Pacific Lines, St. Louis.

Individuals who gave of their knowledge and time include: Barron B. Beshoar, Trinidad; Robert Brown, Stan Brown, Denver; Mrs. Kenneth Cartwright, Lamar; Warren Chandler, Evergreen; C. G. Colgin, Cheyenne, Wyo.; A. Cordova, Garcia; Virginia Miller Cornell, Hideaway Park; Ruth M. Cutter, Grand Valley; Mrs. Arthur De Porter, Carr; Mrs. O. H. Elliott, Glendevey; Mrs. R. B. Fickel, Berthoud; W. R. Foster, McClave; Mrs. Zethyl Gates, Loveland.

Also: Mrs. Bernice Harbert, Woodrow; Werner Helms, Cortez; Miss Hazel Johnson, Greeley; Miss Anne H. Matlack, Longmont; James H. McKinley, Walsenburg; Mrs. Wayne Porter, Redvale; Rev. Donald C. Simonton, Vail; Elizabeth Bowie Snedden, Paonia; Mrs. Floyd Starlin, Akron; Jeanette Faris Thach, Walsenburg; Houston Waring, Littleton; and Betty Woodworth, Fort Collins.

About the author of *Colorado Place Names*: Geo. R. Eichler has a solid writing background. First, as a daily newspaper reporter and editor; now as a public relations counsel, researcher, and editor. A Denver native, he now lives in the Golden area, pursuing varied interests. These include Colorado history, printing, and books (as a Western Americana collector and part-time bookman). And writing: he is researching another place name book, and one on the heritage of miners' candlesticks.